Mastering Python Regular Expressions

Leverage regular expressions in Python even for the most complex features

Félix López

Víctor Romero

[PACKT] open source
PUBLISHING
community experience distilled

BIRMINGHAM - MUMBAI

Mastering Python Regular Expressions

First published: February 2014

Production Reference: 1140214

Published by Packt Publishing Ltd.
Livery Place
35 Livery Street
Birmingham B3 2PB, UK.

ISBN 978-1-78328-315-6

www.packtpub.com

Cover Image by Gagandeep Sharma (er.gagansharma@gmail.com)

Credits

Authors
Félix López
Víctor Romero

Reviewers
Mohit Goenka
Jing (Dave) Tian

Acquisition Editors
James Jones
Mary Jasmine Nadar

Content Development Editor
Rikshith Shetty

Technical Editors
Akashdeep Kundu
Faisal Siddiqui

Copy Editors
Roshni Banerjee
Sarang Chari

Project Coordinator
Sageer Parkar

Proofreader
Linda Morris

Indexer
Priya Subramani

Graphics
Ronak Dhruv
Abhinash Sahu

Production Coordinator
Nitesh Thakur

Cover Work
Nitesh Thakur

About the Authors

Félix López started his career in web development before moving to software in the currency exchange market, where there were a lot of new security challenges. Later, he spent four years creating an IDE to develop games for hundreds of different mobile device OS variations, in addition to creating more than 50 games. Before joining ShuttleCloud, he spent two years working on applications with sensor networks, Arduino, ZigBee, and custom hardware. One example is an application that detects the need for streetlight utilities in major cities based on existing atmospheric brightness. His first experience with Python was seven years ago, He used it for small scripts, web scrapping, and so on. Since then, he has used Python for almost all his projects: websites, standalone applications, and so on. Nowadays, he uses Python along with RabbitMQ in order to integrate services.

He's currently working for ShuttleCloud, an U.S.-based startup, whose technology is used by institutions such as Stanford and Harvard, and companies such as Google.

I would like to thank @panchoHorrillo for helping me with some parts of the book and especially my family for supporting me, despite the fact that I spend most of my time with my work ;)

Víctor Romero currently works as a solutions architect at MuleSoft, Inc. He started his career in the dotcom era and has been a regular contributor to open source software ever since. Originally from the sunny city of Malaga, Spain, his international achievements include integrating the applications present in the cloud storage of a skyscraper in New York City, and creating networks for the Italian government in Rome.

I would like to thank my mom for instilling the love of knowledge in me, my grandmother for teaching me the value of hard work, and the rest of my family for being such an inspiration. I would also like to thank my friends and colleagues for their unconditional support during the creation of this book.

About the Reviewers

Mohit Goenka graduated from the University of Southern California (USC) with an M.Sc. in computer science. His thesis emphasized on Game Theory and Human Behavior concepts as applied in real-world security games. He also received an award for academic excellence from the Office of International Services at USC. He has showcased his presence in various realms of computers, including artificial intelligence, machine learning, path planning, multiagent systems, neural networks, computer vision, computer networks, and operating systems.

During his years as a student, Mohit won multiple competitions cracking codes and presented his work on *Detection of Untouched UFOs* to a wide audience. Not only is he a software developer by profession, but coding is also his hobby. He spends most of his free time learning about new technology and grooming his skills.

What adds a feather to his cap is Mohit's poetic skills. Some of his works are part of the University of Southern California Libraries archive under the cover of *The Lewis Carroll Collection*. In addition to this, he has made significant contributions by volunteering his time to serve the community.

Jing (Dave) Tian is now a graduate research fellow and a Ph.D student in the computer science department at the University of Oregon. He is a member of OSIRIS lab. His research direction involves system security, embedded system security, trusted computing, and static analysis for security and virtualization. He also spent a year on artificial intelligence and machine learning direction, and taught the *Intro to Problem Solving using Python* class in the department. Before that, he worked as a software developer at Linux Control Platform (LCP) group in the Alcatel-Lucent (formerly Lucent Technologies) research and development for around four years. He has got B.S. and M.E. degrees from EE in China.

I would like to thank the author of the book, who has done a good job for both Python and regular expressions. I would also like to thank the editors of the book, who made this book perfect and offered me the opportunity to review such a nice book.

www.PacktPub.com

Support files, eBooks, discount offers and more

You might want to visit www.PacktPub.com for support files and downloads related to your book.

Did you know that Packt offers eBook versions of every book published, with PDF and ePub files available? You can upgrade to the eBook version at www.PacktPub.com and as a print book customer, you are entitled to a discount on the eBook copy. Get in touch with us at service@packtpub.com for more details.

At www.PacktPub.com, you can also read a collection of free technical articles, sign up for a range of free newsletters and receive exclusive discounts and offers on Packt books and eBooks.

http://PacktLib.PacktPub.com

Do you need instant solutions to your IT questions? PacktLib is Packt's online digital book library. Here, you can access, read and search across Packt's entire library of books.

Why Subscribe?

- Fully searchable across every book published by Packt
- Copy and paste, print and bookmark content
- On demand and accessible via web browser

Free Access for Packt account holders

If you have an account with Packt at www.PacktPub.com, you can use this to access PacktLib today and view nine entirely free books. Simply use your login credentials for immediate access.

Table of Contents

Preface

Text processing has been one of the most relevant topics since computer science took its very first baby steps. After a few decades of investigation, we now have one of the most versatile and pervasive tools that exist: regular expressions. Validation, search, extraction, and replacement of text are operations that have been simplified thanks to Regular Expressions.

This book will initially cover regular expressions from a bird's-eye view, proceeding step-by-step to more advanced topics such as regular expression specifics on Python or grouping, workaround, and performance. All the topics will be covered with Python-specific examples that can be used straightaway in the Python console.

What this book covers

Chapter 1, Introducing Regular Expressions, will introduce the basics of the regular expression syntax from a non-Python-specific point of view.

Chapter 2, Regular Expressions with Python, will cover the Python's API for regular expressions and its quirks from a Python-specific point of view.

Chapter 3, Grouping, covers the regular expression functionality to extract portions of information, apply quantifiers to specific parts, and perform correct alternation.

Chapter 4, Look Around, explains the concept of zero-width assertions and the different types of look-around mechanisms.

Chapter 5, Performance of Regular Expressions, will cover different tools to measure the speed of a regular expression, the details of the regular expression module of Python, and different recommendations to improve the performance of regular expressions.

What you need for this book

To understand this book, a basic knowledge of Python in any of the supported platforms is required. It is important to be able to make use of a console with access to the Python command line.

Previous knowledge of regular expressions is not required as it will be covered from scratch.

Who this book is for

This book is intended for Python developers who wish to understand regular expressions in general and also how to leverage them specifically in Python.

Conventions

In this book, you will find a number of styles of text that distinguish between different kinds of information. Here are some examples of these styles, and an explanation of their meaning.

Code words in text, database table names, folder names, filenames, file extensions, pathnames, dummy URLs, user input, and Twitter handles are shown as follows: "We can include other contexts through the use of the `include` directive."

A block of code is set as follows:

```
>>> import re
>>> pattern = re.compile(r'<HTML>')
>>> pattern.match("<HTML>")
```

When we wish to draw your attention to a particular part of a code block, the relevant lines or items are set in bold:

```
>>> import re
>>> pattern = re.compile(r'<HTML>')
>>> pattern.match("<HTML>")
```

New terms and **important words** are shown in bold. Words that you see on the screen, in menus or dialog boxes for example, appear in the text like this: "clicking the **Next** button moves you to the next screen".

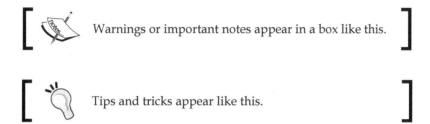

Warnings or important notes appear in a box like this.

Tips and tricks appear like this.

Reader feedback

Feedback from our readers is always welcome. Let us know what you think about this book—what you liked or may have disliked. Reader feedback is important for us to develop titles that you really get the most out of.

To send us general feedback, simply send an e-mail to feedback@packtpub.com, and mention the book title via the subject of your message.If there is a topic that you have expertise in and you are interested in either writing or contributing to a book, see our author guide on www.packtpub.com/authors.

Customer support

Now that you are the proud owner of a Packt book, we have a number of things to help you to get the most from your purchase.

Downloading the example code

You can download the example code files for all Packt books you have purchased from your account at http://www.packtpub.com. If you purchased this book elsewhere, you can visit http://www.packtpub.com/support and register to have the files e-mailed directly to you.

Errata

Although we have taken every care to ensure the accuracy of our content, mistakes do happen. If you find a mistake in one of our books—maybe a mistake in the text or the code—we would be grateful if you would report this to us. By doing so, you can save other readers from frustration and help us improve subsequent versions of this book. If you find any errata, please report them by visiting http://www.packtpub. com/submit-errata, selecting your book, clicking on the **errata submission form** link, and entering the details of your errata. Once your errata are verified, your submission will be accepted and the errata will be uploaded on our website, or added to any list of existing errata, under the Errata section of that title. Any existing errata can be viewed by selecting your title from http://www.packtpub.com/support.

Piracy

Piracy of copyright material on the Internet is an ongoing problem across all media. At Packt, we take the protection of our copyright and licenses very seriously. If you come across any illegal copies of our works, in any form, on the Internet, please provide us with the location address or website name immediately so that we can pursue a remedy.

Please contact us at copyright@packtpub.com with a link to the suspected pirated material.

We appreciate your help in protecting our authors, and our ability to bring you valuable content.

Questions

You can contact us at questions@packtpub.com if you are having a problem with any aspect of the book, and we will do our best to address it.

1
Introducing Regular Expressions

Regular expressions are text patterns that define the form a text string should have. Using them, among other usages, it will be possible to do the following activities:

- Check if an input honors a given pattern; for example, we can check whether a value entered in a HTML formulary is a valid e-mail address
- Look for a pattern appearance in a piece of text; for example, check if either the word "color" or the word "colour" appears in a document with just one scan
- Extract specific portions of a text; for example, extract the postal code of an address
- Replace portions of text; for example, change any appearance of "color" or "colour" with "red"
- Split a larger text into smaller pieces, for example, splitting a text by any appearance of the dot, comma, or newline characters

In this chapter, we are going to learn the basics of regular expressions from a language-agnostic point of view. At the end of the chapter, we will understand how regular expressions work, but we won't yet be able to execute a regular expression in Python. This is going to be covered in the next chapter. Because of this reason, the examples in this chapter will be approached from a theoretical point of view rather than being executed in Python.

History, relevance, and purpose

Regular expressions are pervasive. They can be found in the newest offimatic suite or JavaScript framework to those UNIX tools dating back to the 70s. No modern programming language can be called complete until it supports regular expressions.

Although they are prevalent in languages and frameworks, regular expressions are not yet pervasive in the modern coder's toolkit. One of the reasons often used to explain this is the tough learning curve that they have. Regular expressions can be difficult to master and very complex to read if they are not written with care.

As a result of this complexity, it is not difficult to find in Internet forums the old chestnut:

> *"Some people, when confronted with a problem, think "I know, I'll use regular expressions." Now they have two problems."*

> *-Jamie Zawinski, 1997*

You'll find it at `https://groups.google.com/forum/?hl=en#!msg/alt.religion.emacs/DR057Srw5-c/Co-2L2BKn7UJ`.

Going through this book, we'll learn how to leverage the best practices when writing regular expressions to greatly simplify the reading process.

Even though regular expressions can be found in the latest and greatest programming languages nowadays and will, probably, for many years on, their history goes back to 1943 when the neurophysiologists Warren McCulloch and Walter Pitts published *A logical calculus of the ideas immanent in nervous activity*. This paper not only represented the beginning of the regular expressions, but also proposed the first mathematical model of a neural network.

The next step was taken in 1956, this time by a mathematician. Stephen Kleene wrote the paper *Representation of events in nerve nets and finite automata*, where he coined the terms **regular sets** and **regular expressions**.

Twelve years later, in 1968, a legendary pioneer of computer science took Kleene's work and extended it, publishing his studies in the paper *Regular Expression Search Algorithm*. This engineer was Ken Thompson, known for the design and implementation of Unix, the B programming language, the UTF-8 encoding, and others.

Ken Thompson's work didn't end in just writing a paper. He included support for these regular expressions in his version of QED. To search with a regular expression in QED, the following had to be written:

```
g/<regular expression>/p
```

In the preceding line of code, g means global search and p means print. If, instead of writing `regular expression`, we write the short form re, we get `g/re/p`, and therefore, the beginnings of the venerable UNIX command-line tool `grep`.

The next outstanding milestones were the release of the first non-proprietary library of **regex** by Henry Spence, and later, the creation of the scripting language **Perl** by Larry Wall. Perl pushed the regular expressions to the mainstream.

The implementation in Perl went forward and added many modifications to the original regular expression syntax, creating the so-called **Perl flavor**. Many of the later implementations in the rest of the languages or tools are based on the Perl flavor of regular expressions.

The IEEE thought their POSIX standard has tried to standardize and give better Unicode support to the regular expression syntax and behaviors. This is called the POSIX flavor of the regular expressions.

Today, the standard Python module for regular expressions — re — supports only Perl-style regular expressions. There is an effort to write a new regex module with better POSIX style support at `https://pypi.python.org/pypi/regex`. This new module is intended to replace Python's re module implementation eventually. In this book, we will learn how to leverage only the standard re module.

Regular expressions, regex, regexp, or regexen?

Henry Spencer referred indistinctly to his famous library as "regex" or "regexp". Wikipedia proposed *regex* or *regexp* to be used as abbreviations. The famous Jargon File lists them as *regexp*, regex, and reg-ex.

However, even though there does not seem to be a very strict approach to naming regular expressions, they are based in the field of mathematics called **formal languages**, where being exact is everything. Most modern implementations support features that cannot be expressed in formal languages, and therefore, they are not real regular expressions. Larry Wall, creator of the Perl language, used the term **regexes** or **regexen** for this reason.

In this book, we will indistinctly use all the aforementioned terms as if they were perfect synonyms.

The regular expression syntax

Any experienced developer has undoubtedly used some kind of regular expression. For instance, in the operating system console, it's not uncommon to find the usage of the asterisk (*) or the question mark (?) to find files.

The question mark will match a single character with any value on a filename. For example, a pattern such as `file?.xml` will match `file1.xml`, `file2.xml`, and `file3.xml`, but it won't match `file99.xml` as the pattern expresses that anything that starts with `file`, followed by just one character of any value, and ends with `.xml`, will be matched.

A similar meaning is defined for asterisk (*). When asterisk is used, any number of characters with any value is accepted. In the case of `file*.xml`, anything that starts with `file`, followed by any number of characters of any value, and finishes with `.xml`, will be matched.

In this expression, we can find two kind of components: **literals** (`file` and `.xml`) and **metacharacters** (? or *). The regular expressions we will learn in this book are much more powerful than the simple patterns we can typically find on the operating system command line, but both can share one single definition:

A regular expression is a pattern of text that consists of ordinary characters (for example, letters *a* through *z* or numbers *0* through *9*) and special characters known as metacharacters. This pattern describes the strings that would match when applied to a text.

Let's see our very first regular expression that will match any word starting with ⋯▸a:

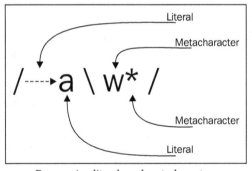

Regex using literals and metacharacters

Representation of regular expressions in this book

In the following figures of this book, regular expressions are going to be represented bounded by the / symbol. This is the QED demarcation that is followed in most of the text books. The code examples, however, won't use this notation.

On the other hand, even with monospaced font faces, the white spaces of a regular expression are difficult to count. In order to simplify the reading, every single whitespace in the figures will appear as ⋯▸.

The previous regular expression is again using literals and metacharacters. The literals here are ⋯▸ and a, and the metacharacters are \ and w that match any alphanumeric character including underscore, and *, that will allow any number of repetitions of the previous character, and therefore, any number of repetitions of any word character, including underscore.

We will cover the metacharacters later in this chapter, but let's start by understanding the literals.

Literals

Literals are the simplest form of pattern matching in regular expressions. They will simply succeed whenever that literal is found.

If we apply the regular expression /fox/ to search the phrase The quick brown fox jumps over the lazy dog, we will find one match:

```
The-▸quick-▸brown-▸fox-▸jumps-▸over-▸the-▸lazy-▸dog

/ fox /
```

Searching using a regular expression

However, we can also obtain several results instead of just one, if we apply the regular expression /be/ to the following phrase To be, or not to be:

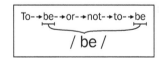

Multiple results searching with regex

We have just learned in the previous section that metacharacters can coexist with literals in the same expression. Because of this coexistence, we can find that some expressions do not mean what we intended. For example, if we apply the expression `/(this is inside)/` to search the text `this is outside (this is inside)`, we will find that the parentheses are not included in the result. This happens because parentheses are metacharacters and they have a special meaning.

Incorrectly unescaped metacharacters

We can use metacharacters as if they were literals. There are three mechanisms to do so:

- Escape the metacharacters by preceding them with a backslash.
- In python, use the `re.escape` method to escape non-alphanumeric characters that may appear in the expression. We will cover this in *Chapter 2, Regular Expressions with Python.*
- **Quoting with \Q and \E:** There is a third mechanism to quote in regular expressions, the quoting with \Q and \E. In the flavors that support them, it's as simple as enclosing the parts that have to be quoted with \Q (which starts a quote) and \E (which ends it).

However, this is not supported in Python at the moment.

Using the backslash method, we can convert the previous expression to `/\(this is inside\)/` and apply it again to the same text to have the parentheses included in the result:

Escaped metacharacters in regex

In regular expressions, there are twelve metacharacters that should be escaped if they are to be used with their literal meaning:

- Backslash \
- Caret ^
- Dollar sign $
- Dot .

- Pipe symbol |
- Question mark ?
- Asterisk *
- Plus sign +
- Opening parenthesis (
- Closing parenthesis)
- Opening square bracket [
- The opening curly brace {

In some cases, the regular expression engines will do their best to understand if they should have a literal meaning even if they are not escaped; for example, the opening curly brace { will only be treated as a metacharacter if it's followed by a number to indicate a repetition, as we will learn later in this chapter.

Character classes

We are going to use a metacharacter for the first time to learn how to leverage the character classes. The character classes (also known as character sets) allow us to define a character that will match if any of the defined characters on the set is present.

To define a character class, we should use the opening square bracket metacharacter [, then any accepted characters, and finally close with a closing square bracket]. For instance, let's define a regular expression that can match the word "license" in British and American English written form:

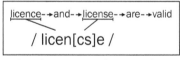

Searching using a character class

It is possible to also use the range of a character. This is done by leveraging the hyphen symbol (-) between two related characters; for example, to match any lowercase letter we can use [a-z]. Likewise, to match any single digit we can define the character set [0-9].

The character classes' ranges can be combined to be able to match a character against many ranges by just putting one range after the other—no special separation is required. For instance, if we want to match any lowercase or uppercase alphanumeric character, we can use `[0-9a-zA-Z]` (see next table for a more detailed explanation). This can be alternatively written using the union mechanism: `[0-9[a-z[A-Z]]]`.

Element	Description
[	Matches the following set of characters
0-9	Matches anything between 0 and 9 (0, 1, 2, 3, 4, 5, 6, 7, 8, 9).
	Or
a-z	Matches anything between a and z (a, b, c, d, ..., z)
	Or
A-Z	Matches anything between A and Z (A, B, C, D, ..., Z)
]	End of character set

There is another possibility—the negation of ranges. We can invert the meaning of a character set by placing a caret (^) symbol right after the opening square bracket metacharacter ([). If we have a character class such as `[0-9]` meaning any digit, the negated character class `[^0-9]` will match anything that is not a digit. However, it is important to notice that there has to be a character that is not a digit; for example, `/hello[^0-9]/` won't match the string `hello` because after the ⋯→ there has to be a non-digit character. There is a mechanism to do this—called **negative lookahead**—and it will be covered in *Chapter 4, Look Around*.

Predefined character classes

After using character classes for some time, it becomes clear that some of them are very useful and probably worthy of a shortcut.

Luckily enough, there are a number of predefined character classes that can be re-used and will be already known by other developers, making the expressions using them more readable.

These characters are not only useful as well-known shortcuts for typical character sets, but also have different meanings in different contexts. The character class \w, which matches any alphanumeric character, will match a different set of characters depending on the configured locale and the support of Unicode.

The following table shows the character classes supported at this moment in Python:

Element	Description (for regex with default flags)
.	This element matches any character except newline \n
\d	This matches any decimal digit; this is equivalent to the class [0-9]
\D	This matches any non-digit character; this is equivalent to the class [^0-9]
\s	This matches any whitespace character; this is equivalent to the class [⋯→\t\n\r\f\v]
\S	This matches any non-whitespace character; this is equivalent to the class [^ \t\n\r\f\v]
\w	This matches any alphanumeric character; this is equivalent to the class [a-zA-Z0-9_]
\W	This matches any non-alphanumeric character; this is equivalent to the class [^a-zA-Z0-9_]

POSIX character classes in Python

The POSIX standard provides a number of character classes' denominations, for example, [:alnum:] for alphanumeric characters, [:alpha:] for alphabetic characters, or [:space:] for all whitespace characters, including line breaks.

All the POSIX character classes follow the same [:name:] notation, rendering them easily identifiable. However, they are not supported in Python at the moment.

If you come across one of them, you can implement the same functionality by leveraging the character classes' functionalities we just studied in this section. As an example, for an ASCII equivalent of [:alnum:] with an English locale, we can write [a-zA-Z0-9].

The first one from the previous table — the dot — requires special attention. The dot is probably one of the oldest and also one of the most used metacharacters. The dot can match any character except a newline character.

The reason to not match the newline is probably UNIX. In UNIX, the command-line tools usually worked line by line, and the regular expressions available at the moment were applied separately to those lines. Therefore, there were no newline characters to match.

Let's put the dot in practice by creating a regular expression that matches three characters of any value except newline:

/.../

Element	Description
.	Matches any character
.	Matches any character followed by the previous one
.	Matches any character followed by the previous one

The dot is a very powerful metacharacter that can create problems if it is not used moderately. In most of the cases where the dot is used, it could be considered overkill (or just a symptom of laziness when writing regular expressions).

To better define what is expected to be matched and to express more concisely to any ulterior reader what a regular expression is intended to do, the usage of character classes is much recommended. For instance, when working with Windows and UNIX file paths, to match any character except the slash or the backslash, you can use a negated character set:

[^\/\]

Element	Description
[	Matches a set of characters
^	Not matching this symbol's following characters
\/	Matches a / character
\	Matches a \ character
]	End of the set

This character set is explicitly telling you that we intend to match anything but a Windows or UNIX file path separator.

Alternation

We have just learned how to match a single character from a set of characters. Now, we are going to learn a broader approach: how to match against a set of regular expressions. This is accomplished using the pipe symbol |.

Let's start by saying that we want to match either if we find the word "yes" or the word "no". Using alternation, it will be as simple as:

```
/yes|no/
```

Element	Description
	Matches either of the following character sets
yes	The characters y, e, and s.
|	Or
no	The characters n and o.

On the other hand, if we want to accept more than two values, we can continue adding values to the alternation like this:

```
/yes|no|maybe/
```

Element	Description
	Matches either of the following character sets
yes	The literal "yes"
|	Or
no	The literal "no"
|	Or
maybe	The literal "maybe"

When using in bigger regular expressions, we will probably need to wrap our alternation inside parentheses to express that only that part is alternated and not the whole expression. For instance, if we make the mistake of not using the parentheses, as in the following expression:

```
/Licence: yes|no/
```

Element	Description
	Matches either of the following character sets
Licence: yes	The characters L, i, c, e, n, c, e, :, ⋯→, y, e, and s
		Or
no	The characters n and o.

We may think we are accepting either Licence: yes or Licence: no, but we are actually accepting either Licence: yes or no as the alternation has been applied to the whole regular expression instead of just the yes|no part. A correct approach for this will be:

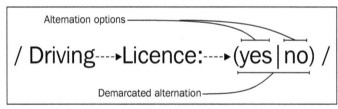

Regular expression using alternation

Quantifiers

So far, we have learned how to define a single character in a variety of fashions. At this point, we will leverage the quantifiers — the mechanisms to define how a character, metacharacter, or character set can be repeated.

For instance, if we define that a \d can be repeated many times, we can easily create a form validator for the `number of items` field of a shopping cart (remember that \d matches any decimal digit). But let's start from the beginning, the three basic quantifiers: the question mark ?, the plus sign +, and the asterisk *.

Symbol	Name	Quantification of previous character
?	Question mark	Optional (0 or 1 repetitions)
*	Asterisk	Zero or more times
+	Plus sign	One or more times
{n,m}	Curly braces	Between *n* and *m* times

In the preceding table, we can find the three basic quantifiers, each with a specific utility. The question mark can be used to match the word `car` and its plural form `cars`:

`/cars?/`

Element	Description
car	Matches the characters c, a, r and s
s?	Optionally matches the character s

In the previous example, the question mark is only applied to the character s and not to the whole word. The quantifiers are always applied only to the previous token.

Another interesting example of the usage of the question mark quantifier will be to match a telephone number that can be in the format 555-555-555, 555 555 555, or 555555555.

We now know how to leverage character sets to accept different characters, but is it possible to apply a quantifier to a character set? Yes, quantifiers can be applied to characters, character sets, and even to groups (a feature we will cover in *Chapter 3, Grouping*). We can construct a regular expression like this to validate the telephone numbers:

`/\d+[-\s]?\d+[-\s]?\d+/`

In the next table, we can find a detailed explanation of the preceding regular expression:

Element	Type	Description
\d	Predefined character set	Any decimal character
+	Quantifier	- that is repeated one or more times
[-\s]	Character set	A hyphen or whitespace character
?	Quantifier	- that may or may not appear
\d	Predefined character set	Any decimal character
+	Quantifier	- that is repeated one or more times
[-\s]	Character set	A hyphen or whitespace character
\d	Predefined character set	Any decimal character
+	Quantifier	- that is repeated one or more times

At the beginning of this section, one more kind of quantifier using the curly braces had been mentioned. Using this syntax, we can define that the previous character must appear exactly three times by appending it with {3}, that is, the expression \w{8} specifies exactly eight alphanumeric digits.

We can also define a certain range of repetitions by providing a minimum and maximum number of repetitions, that is, between three and eight times can be defined with the syntax {4,7}. Either the minimum or the maximum value can be omitted defaulting to 0 and infinite respectively. To designate a repetition of up to three times, we can use {,3}, we can also establish a repetition at least three times with {3,}.

Readability Tip

Instead of using {,1}, you can use the question mark. The same applies to {0,} for the asterisk * and {1,} for the plus sign +.

Other developers will expect you to do so. If you don't follow this practice, anyone reading your expressions will lose some time trying to figure out what kind of fancy stuff you tried to accomplish.

These four different combinations are shown in the next table:

Syntax	Description
{n}	The previous character is repeated exactly *n* times.
{n, }	The previous character is repeated at least *n* times.
{,n}	The previous character is repeated at most *n* times.
{n,m}	The previous character is repeated between *n* and *m* times (both inclusive).

Earlier in this chapter, we created a regular expression to validate telephone numbers that can be in the format 555-555-555, 555 555 555, or 555555555. We defined a regular expression to validate it using the metacharacter plus sign: /\d+[-\s]?\d+[-\s]?\d+/. It will require the digits (\d) to be repeated one or more times.

Let's fine-tune the regular expression by defining that the leftmost digit group can contain up to three characters, while the rest of the digit groups should contain exactly three digits:

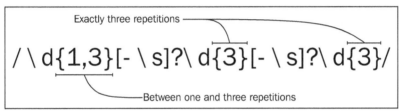

Using quantifiers

Greedy and reluctant quantifiers

We still haven't defined what would match if we apply a quantifier such as this /".+"/ to a text such as the following: English "Hello", Spanish "Hola". We may expect that it matches "Hello" and "Hola" but it will actually match "Hello", Spanish "Hola".

This behavior is called greedy and is one of the two possible behaviors of the quantifiers in Python: **greedy** and **non-greedy** (also known as **reluctant**).

- The greedy behavior of the quantifiers is applied by default in the quantifiers. A greedy quantifier will try to match as much as possible to have the biggest match result possible.

- The non-greedy behavior can be requested by adding an extra question mark to the quantifier; for example, ??, *? or +?. A quantifier marked as reluctant will behave like the exact opposite of the greedy ones. They will try to have the smallest match possible.

Possessive quantifiers

There is a third behavior of the quantifiers, the possessive behavior. This behavior is only supported by the Java and .NET flavors of the regular expressions at the moment.

They are represented with an extra plus symbol to the quantifier; for example, ?+, *+, or ++. Possessive quantifiers won't have further coverage in this book.

We can understand better how this quantifier works by looking at the next figure. We will apply almost the same regular expression (with the exception of leaving the quantifier as greedy or marking it as reluctant) to the same text, having two very different results:

```
                    / ".+" /
English-→"Hello",-→Spanish-→"Hola".
                    / ".+?" /
```

Greedy and reluctant quantifiers

Boundary Matchers

Until this point, we have just tried to find out regular expressions within a text. Sometimes, when it is required to match a whole line, we may also need to match at the beginning of a line or even at the end. This can be done thanks to the **boundary matchers**.

The boundary matchers are a number of identifiers that will correspond to a particular position inside of the input. The following table shows the boundary matchers available in Python:

Matcher	Description
^	Matches at the beginning of a line
$	Matches at the end of a line
\b	Matches a word boundary
\B	Matches the opposite of \b. Anything that is not a word boundary
\A	Matches the beginning of the input
\Z	Matches the end of the input

These boundary matchers will behave differently in different contexts. For instance, the word boundaries (\b) will depend directly on the configured locale as different languages may have different word boundaries, and the beginning and end of line boundaries will behave differently based on certain flags that we will study in the next chapter.

Let's start working with boundary matchers by writing a regular expression that will match lines that start with "Name:". If you take a look at the previous table, you may notice the existence of the metacharacter ^ that expresses the beginning of a line. Using it, we can write the following expression:

```
/^Name:/
```

Element	Description
^	Matches the beginning of the line
N	Matches the followed by character N
a	Matches the followed by character a
m	Matches the followed by character m
e	Matches the followed by character e
:	Matches the followed by symbol colon

If we want to take one step further and continue using the caret and the dollar sign in combination to match the end of the line, we should take into consideration that from now on we are going to be matching against the whole line, and not just trying to find a pattern within a line.

Following the previous example, let's say that we want to make sure that after the name, there are only alphabetic characters or spaces until the end of the line. We will do this by matching the whole line until the end by setting a character set with the accepted characters and allowing their repetition any number of times until the end of the line.

```
/^Name:[\sa-zA-Z]+$/
```

Element	Description
^	Matches the beginning of the line.
N	Matches the followed by character N.
a	Matches the followed by character a.
m	Matches the followed by character m.
e	Matches the followed by character e.
:	Matches the followed by colon symbol.
[\sa-zA-Z]	Then matches the followed by whitespace, or any alphabetic lowercase or uppercase character.
+	The character can be repeated one or more times.
$	Until the end of the line.

Another outstanding boundary matcher is the word boundary \b. It will match any character that is not a word character (in the configured locale), and therefore, any potential word boundary. This is very useful when we want to work with isolated words and we don't want to create character sets with every single character that may divide our words (spaces, commas, colons, hyphens, and so on). We can, for instance, make sure that the word hello appears in a text by using the following regular expression:

```
/\bhello\b/
```

Element	Description
\b	Matches a word boundary.
h	Matches the followed by character h.
e	Matches the followed by character e.
l	Matches the followed by character l.
l	Matches the followed by character l.
o	Matches the followed by character o.
\b	Then matches another followed by word boundary.

As an exercise, we could think why the preceding expression is better than /hello/. The reason is that this expression will match an isolated word instead of a word containing "hello", that is, /hello/ will easily match hello, helloed, or Othello; while /\bhello\b/ will only match hello.

Summary

In this first chapter, we have learned the importance of the regular expressions and how they became such a relevant tool for the programmers.

We also studied from a yet non-practical point of view, the basic regular expression syntax and some of the key features, such as character classes and quantifiers.

In the next chapter, we are going to jump over to Python to start practicing with the re module.

2
Regular Expressions with Python

In the previous chapter, we've seen how generic regular expressions work. In this chapter, we walk you through all the operations Python provides us with to work with regular expressions and how Python deals with them.

To do so, we will see the quirks of the language when dealing with regular expressions, the different types of strings, the API it offers through the `RegexObject` and `MatchObject` classes, every operation that we can do with them in depth with many examples, as well as some problems generally faced by users. Lastly, we will see the small nuances and differences between Python and other regex engines and between Python 2 and Python 3.

A brief introduction

Since v1.5, Python provides a Perl-style regular expression with some subtle exceptions that we will see later. Both patterns and strings to be searched can be **Unicode** strings, as well as an 8-bit string (**ASCII**).

Unicode is the universal encoding with more than 110.00 characters and 100 scripts to represent all the world's living characters and even historic scripts. You can think of it as a mapping between numbers, or code points as they are called, and characters. So, we can represent every character, no matter in what language, with one single number. For example, the character 是 is the number 26159, and it is represented as \u662f (hexadecimal) in Python.

Regular expressions are supported by the re module. So, as with all modules in Python, we only need to import it to start playing with them. For that, we need to start the Python interactive shell using the following line of code:

```
>>> import re
```

Once we have imported the module, we can start trying to match a pattern. To do so, we need to compile a pattern, transforming it into **bytecode**, as shown in the following line of code. This bytecode will be executed later by an engine written in C.

```
>>> pattern = re.compile(r'\bfoo\b')
```

 Bytecode is an intermediary language. It's the output generated by languages, which will be later interpreted by an interpreter. The Java bytecode that is interpreted by JVM is probably the best known example.

Once we have the compiled pattern, we can try to match it against a string, as in the following code:

```
>>> pattern.match("foo bar")
<_sre.SRE_Match at 0x108acac60>
```

As we mentioned in the preceding example, we compiled a pattern and then we searched whether the pattern matches the text *foo bar*.

Working with Python and regular expressions in the command line is easy enough to perform quick tests. You just need to start the python interpreter and import the re module as we mentioned previously. However, if you prefer a GUI to test your regex, you can download one written in Python at the following link:

http://svn.python.org/view/*checkout*/python/trunk/Tools/scripts/redemo.py?content-type=text%2Fplain

There are a number of online tools such as the one at https://pythex.org/, as well as desktop programs such as RegexBuddy that we will cover in *Chapter 5, Performance of Regular Expressions.*

At this point, it's preferable to use the interpreter to gain fluency with them and get direct feedback.

Backslash in string literals

Regular expressions aren't part of the core Python language. Thus, there isn't a special syntax for them and therefore they are handled as any other string. As we've seen in *Chapter 1, Introducing Regular Expressions*, the backslash character \ is used to indicate metacharacters or special forms in regular expressions. The backslash is also used in strings to escape special characters. In other words, it has a special meaning in Python. So, if we need to use the \ character, we'll have to escape it: \\. This will give the string literal meaning to the backslash. However, in order to match inside a regular expression, we should escape the backslashes, effectively writing four back slashes: \\\\.

Just as an example, let's write a regular expression to match \:

```
>>> pattern = re.compile("\\\\")
>>> pattern.match("\\author")
<_sre.SRE_Match at 0x104a88e68>
```

As you can see, this is tedious and difficult to understand when the pattern is long.

Python provides the **raw string notation** r, with which the backslashes are treated as normal characters. So, r"\b" is not the backspace anymore; it's just the character \ and the character b, and the same goes for r"\n".

Python 2.x and Python 3.x treat strings differently. In Python 2, there are two types of Strings, 8-bit Strings and Unicode strings; while in Python 3, we have text and binary data. Text is always Unicode and the encoded Unicode is represented as binary data (http://docs.python.org/3.0/whatsnew/3.0.html#text-vs-data-instead-of-unicode-vs-8-bit).

Strings have special notation to indicate what type we're using.

String Python 2.x

Type	Prefixed	Description
String		String literals. They're encoded automatically by using the default encoding (UTF-8 in our case). The backslash is necessary to escape meaningful characters.
		`>>>"España \n"`
		`'Espa\xc3\xb1a \n'`

Type	Prefixed	Description
Raw string	r or R	They're equal to literal strings with the exception of the backslashes, which are treated as normal characters.
		`>>>r"España \n"` `'Espa\xc3\xb1a \\n'`
Unicode string	u or U	These strings use the Unicode character set (ISO 10646).
		`>>>u"España \n"` `u'Espa\xf1a \n'`
Unicode raw string	ur or UR	They're Unicode strings but treat backslashes as normal raw strings.
		`>>>ur"España \n"` `u'Espa\xf1a \\n'`

Go to the *What's new in Python 3* section to find out how the notation is in Python 3

Using raw string is the recommended option following the Python official documentation, and that's what we will be using with Python 2.7 throughout the book. So with this in mind, we can rewrite the regex as follows:

```
>>> pattern = re.compile(r"\\")
>>> pattern.match(r"\author")
<_sre.SRE_Match at 0x104a88f38>
```

Building blocks for Python regex

In Python, there are two different objects dealing with Regex:

- `RegexObject`: It is also known as *Pattern Object*. It represents a compiled regular expression
- `MatchObject`: It represents the matched pattern

RegexObject

In order to start matching patterns, we'll have to compile the regex. Python gives us an interface to do that as we've seen previously. The result will be a pattern object or `RegexObject`. This object has several methods for typical operations on regular expressions. As we will see later, the re module provides a shorthand for every operation so that we can avoid compiling it first.

```
>>> pattern = re.compile(r'fo+')
```

The compilation of a regular expression produces a reusable pattern object that provides all the operations that can be done, such as matching a pattern and finding all substrings that match a particular regex. So, for example, if we want to know if a string starts with <HTML>, we can use the following code:

```
>>> pattern = re.compile(r'<HTML>')
>>> pattern.match("<HTML>")
   <_sre.SRE_Match at 0x108076578>
```

There are two ways of matching patterns and executing the operations related to the regular expressions. We can compile a pattern, which gives us a RegexObject, or we can use the module operations. Let's compare the two different mechanisms in the following examples.

If we want to re-use the regular expression, we can use the following code:

```
>>> pattern = re.compile(r'<HTML>')
>>> pattern.match("<HTML>")
```

On the other hand, we can directly perform the operation on the module using the following line of code:

```
>>> re.match(r'<HTML>', "<HTML>")
```

The re module provides a wrapper for every operation in the RegexObject. You can see them as shortcuts.

Internally, these wrappers create the RegexObject and then call the corresponding method. You might be wondering whether every time you call one of these wrappers it compiles the regular expression first. The answer is no. The re module caches the compiled pattern so that in future calls it doesn't have to compile it again.

Beware of the memory needs of your program. When you're using module operations, you don't control the cache, and so you can end up with a lot of memory usage. You can always use re.purge to clear the cache but this is a tradeoff with performance. Using compiled patterns allows you to have a fine-grained control of the memory consumption because you can decide when to purge them.

There are some differences between both ways though. With the RegexObject, it is possible to limit the region in which the pattern will be searched, for example limit the search of a pattern between the characters at index 2 and 20. In addition to that, you can set flags in every call by using the operations in the module. However, be careful; every time you change the flag, a new pattern will be compiled and cached.

Let's dive into the most important operations that can be done with a pattern object.

Searching

Let's see the operations we have to look for patterns in strings. Note that python has two operations, match and search; where many other languages have one, match.

match(string[, pos[, endpos]])

This method tries to match the compiled pattern only at the beginning of the string. If there is a match, then it returns a `MatchObject`. So, for example, let's try to match whether a string starts with `<HTML>` or not:

```
>>> pattern = re.compile(r'<HTML>')
>>> pattern.match("<HTML><head>")
<_sre.SRE_Match at 0x108076578>
```

In the preceding example, first we've compiled the pattern and then we've found a match in the `<HTML><head>` string.

Let's see what happens when the string doesn't start with `<HTML>`, as shown in the following lines of code:

```
>>> pattern.match("···><HTML>")
    None
```

As you can see, there is no match. Remember what we said before, match tries to match at the beginning of the string. The string starts with a whitespace unlike the pattern. Note the difference with search in the following example:

```
>>> pattern.search("···><HTML>")
<_sre.SRE_Match at 0x108076578>
```

As expected, we have a match.

The optional **pos** parameter specifies where to start searching, as shown in the following code:

```
>>> pattern = re.compile(r'<HTML>')
>>> pattern.match("···>···><HTML>")
    None
>>> pattern.match("···>···><HTML>", 2)
    <_sre.SRE_Match at 0x1043bc850>
```

In the highlighted code, we can see how the pattern has a match even though there are two whitespaces in the string. This is possible because we've set **pos** to 2, so the match operation starts searching in that position.

Note that **pos** bigger than 0 doesn't mean that string starts at that index, for example:

```
>>> pattern = re.compile(r'^<HTML>')
>>> pattern.match("<HTML>")
   <_sre.SRE_Match at 0x1043bc8b8>
>>> pattern.match("⋯⋯<HTML>",  2)
   None
```

In the preceding code, we've created a pattern to match strings in which the first character after "start" is followed by <HTML>. After that, we've tried to match the string <HTML> starting at the second character, <. There is no match because the pattern is trying to match the ^ metacharacter at the 2 position first.

Anchor characters tip

The characters ^ and $ indicate the start and end of the string respectively. You can neither see them in the strings nor write them, but they are always there and are valid characters for the regex engine.

Note the different result if we slice the string 2 positions, as in the following code:

```
>>> pattern.match("⋯⋯<HTML>"[2:])
   <_sre.SRE_Match at 0x1043bca58>
```

The slice gives us a new string; therefore, there is a ^ metacharacter in it. On the contrary, **pos** just moves the index to the starting point for the search in the string.

The second argument, **endpos**, sets how far the pattern will try to match in the string. In the following case, it's equivalent to slicing:

```
>>> pattern = re.compile(r'<HTML>')
>>> pattern.match("<HTML>"[:2])
   None
>>> pattern.match("<HTML>", 0, 2)
   None
```

So, in the following case, we don't have the problem mentioned with **pos**. There is a match even when the $ metacharacter is used:

```
>>> pattern = re.compile(r'<HTML>$')
>>> pattern.match("<HTML>⋯", 0,6)
<_sre.SRE_Match object at 0x1007033d8>
>>> pattern.match("<HTML>⋯"[:6])
<_sre.SRE_Match object at 0x100703370>
```

As you can see, there is no difference between slicing and **endpos**.

search(string[, pos[, endpos]])

This operation would be like the **match** of many languages, Perl for example.
It tries to match the pattern at any location of the string and not just at the beginning.
If there is a match, it returns a MatchObject.

```
>>> pattern = re.compile(r"world")
>>> pattern.search("hello⇢world")
    <_sre.SRE_Match at 0x1080901d0>
>>> pattern.search("hola⇢mundo ")
    None
```

The **pos** and **endpos** parameters have the same meaning as that in the match operation.

Note that with the MULTILINE flag, the ^ symbol matches at the beginning of the string and at the beginning of each line (we'll see more on this flag later). So, it changes the behavior of search.

In the following example, the first search matches <HTML> because it's at the beginning of the string, but the second search doesn't match because the string starts with a whitespace. And finally, in the third search, we have a match as we find <HTML> right after new line, thanks to re.MULTILINE.

```
>>> pattern = re.compile(r'^<HTML>', re.MULTILINE)
>>> pattern.search("<HTML>")
    <_sre.SRE_Match at 0x1043d3100>
>>> pattern.search("⇢<HTML>")
    None
>>> pattern.search("⇢ ⇢\n<HTML>")
    <_sre.SRE_Match at 0x1043bce68>
```

So, as long as the **pos** parameter is less than, or equal to, the new lines, there will be a match.

```
>>> pattern.search("⇢ ⇢\n<HTML>",  3)
  <_sre.SRE_Match at 0x1043bced0>
>>> pattern.search('</div></body>\n<HTML>', 4)
  <_sre.SRE_Match at 0x1036d77e8>
>>> pattern.search("  \n<HTML>", 4)
    None
```

findall(string[, pos[, endpos]])

The previous operations worked with one match at a time. On the contrary, in this case it returns a list with all the non-overlapping occurrences of a pattern and not the `MatchObject` like `search` and `match` do.

In the following example, we're looking for every word in a string. So, we obtain a list in which every item is the pattern found, in this case a word.

```
>>> pattern = re.compile(r"\w+")
>>> pattern.findall("hello⋯→world")
    ['hello', 'world']
```

Keep in mind that empty matches are a part of the result:

```
>>> pattern = re.compile(r'a*')
>>> pattern.findall("aba")
    ['a', '', 'a', '']
```

I bet you're wondering what's happening here? The trick comes from the `*` quantifier, which allows 0 or more repetitions of the preceding regex; the same had happened with the `?` quantifier.

```
>>> pattern = re.compile(r'a?')
>>> pattern.findall("aba")
    ['a', '', 'a', '']
```

Basically, both of them match the expression even though the preceding regex is not found:

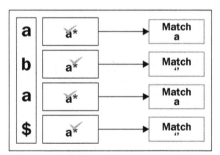

findall matching process

First, the regex matches the character a, then it follows with b. There is a match due to the `*` quantifier, the empty string. After that, it matches another a and finally it tries to match $. As we've mentioned before, even though you can't see $, it's a valid character for the regex engine. As it happened with the b, it matches due to the `*` quantifier.

We've seen quantifiers in depth in *Chapter 1*, *Introducing Regular Expressions*.

In case there are groups in the pattern, they are returned as tuples. The string is scanned from left to right, so the groups are returned in the same order they are found.

The following example tries to match a pattern made of two words and creates a group for every word. That's why we have a list of tuples in which every tuple has two groups.

```
>>> pattern = re.compile(r"(\w+) (\w+)")
>>> pattern.findall("Hello-→world-→hola-→mundo")
    [('Hello', 'world'), ('hola', 'mundo')]
```

The `findall` operation along with `groups` is another thing that seems to confuse a lot of people. In *Chapter 3*, *Groups*, we've dedicated a complete section to explain this complex subject.

finditer(string[, pos[, endpos]])

Its working is essentially the same as `findall`, but it returns an iterator in which each element is a `MatchObject`, so we can use the operations provided by this object. So, it's quite useful when you need information for every match, for example the position in which the substring was matched. Several times, I've found myself using it to understand what's happening in `findall`.

Let's go back to one of our initial examples. Match every two words and capture them:

```
>>> pattern = re.compile(r"(\w+) (\w+)")
>>> it = pattern.finditer("Hello-→world-→hola-→mundo")
>>> match = it.next()
>>> match.groups()
    ('Hello', 'world')
>>> match.span()
    (0, 11)
```

In the preceding example, we can see how we get an iterator with all the matches. For every element in the iterator, we get a `MatchObject`, so we can see the captured groups in the pattern, two in this case. We will also get the position of the match.

```
>>> match = it.next()
>>> match.groups()
    ('hola', 'mundo')
>>> match.span()
    (12, 22)
```

Now, we consume another element from the iterator and perform the same operations as before. So, we get the next match, its groups, and the position of the match. We've done the same as we did with the first match:

```
>>> match = it.next()
Traceback (most recent call last):
  File "<stdin>", line 1, in <module>
StopIteration
```

Finally, we try to consume another match, but in this case a `StopIteration` exception is thrown. This is normal behavior to indicate that there are no more elements.

Modifying a string

In this section, we're going to see the operations to modify strings, such as an operation to divide the string and another to replace some parts of it.

split(string, maxsplit=0)

In almost every language, you can find the `split` operation in strings. The big difference is that the split in the `re` module is more powerful due to which you can use a regex. So, in this case, the string is split based on the matches of the pattern. As always, the best way to understand it is with an example, so let's split a string into lines:

```
>>> re.split(r"\n", "Beautiful⸱is better⸱than⸱ugly.\nExplicit⸱is⸱be
tter⸱than⸱implicit.")

['Beautiful⸱is⸱better⸱than⸱ugly.', 'Explicit⸱is⸱better⸱than⸱impli
cit.']
```

In the preceding example, the match is \n; so, the string is split using it as the separator. Let's see a more complex example of how to get the words in a string:

```
>>> pattern = re.compile(r"\W")
>>> pattern.split("hello⸱world")
['Hello', 'world']
```

In the preceding example, we've defined a pattern to match any non-alphanumeric character. So, in this case the match happens in the whitespace. That's why the string is split into words. Let's see another example to understand it better:

```
>>> pattern = re.compile(r"\W")
>>> pattern.findall("hello⸱world")
['⸱']
```

Note that the match is the whitespace.

The **maxsplit** parameter specifies how many splits can be done at maximum and returns the remaining part in the result:

```
>>> pattern = re.compile(r"\W")
>>> pattern.split("Beautiful is better than ugly", 2)
['Beautiful', 'is', 'better than ugly']
```

As you can see, only two words are split and the other words are a part of the result.

Have you realized that the pattern matched is not included? Take a look at every example in this section. What can we do if we want to capture the pattern too?

The answer is to use groups:

```
>>> pattern = re.compile(r"(-)")
>>> pattern.split("hello-word")
['hello', '-', 'word']
```

This happens because the split operation always returns the captured groups.

Note that when a group matches the start of the string, the result will contain the empty string as a first result:

```
>>> pattern = re.compile(r"(\W)")
>>> pattern.split("→hello→word")
['', '→', 'hello', '→', 'word']
```

sub(repl, string, count=0)

This operation returns the resulting string after replacing the matched pattern in the original string with the replacement. If the pattern is not found, the original string is returned. For example, we're going to replace the digits in the string with - (dash):

```
>>> pattern = re.compile(r"[0-9]+")
>>> pattern.sub("-", "order0→order1→order13")
'order-→order-→order-'
```

Basically, the regex matches 1 and more digits and replaces the pattern matched, 0, 1, and 13 here, with - (dash).

Note that it replaces the leftmost non-overlapping occurrences of the pattern. Let's see another example:

```
>>> re.sub('00', '-', 'order00000')
'order--0'
```

In the preceding example, we're replacing zeroes two by two. So, the first two are matched and then replaced, then the following two zeroes are matched and replaced too, and finally the last zero is left intact.

The `repl` argument can also be a function, in which case it receives a MatchObject as an argument and the string returned is the replacement. For example, imagine you have a legacy system in which there are two kinds of orders. Some start with a dash and the others start with a letter:

- -1234
- A193, B123, C124

You must change it to the following:

- A1234
- B193, B123, B124

In short, the ones starting with a dash should start with an A and the rest should start with a B.

```
>>>def normalize_orders(matchobj):
       if matchobj.group(1) == '-': return "A"
       else: return "B"

>>> re.sub('([-|A-Z])', normalize_orders, '-1234···→A193···→ B123')
'A1234···→B193···→B123'
```

As mentioned previously, for each matched pattern the `normalize_orders` function is called. So, if the first matched group is a –, then we return an A; in any other case, we return B.

Note that in the code we get the first group with the index 1; take a look at the `group` operation to understand why.

Backreferences, a powerful feature is also provided by `sub`. We'll see them in depth in the next chapter. Basically, what it does is that it replaces the backreferences with the corresponding groups. For example, let's say you want to transform markdown to HTML, for the sake of keeping the example short, just bold the text:

```
>>> text = "imagine···→a···→new···→*world*, ···→a···→magic···→*world*"
>>> pattern = re.compile(r'\*(.*?)\*')
>>> pattern.sub(r"<b>\g<1><\\b>", text)
'imagine···→a···→new···→<b>world<\\b>, ···→a···→magic···→<b>world<\\b>'
```

As always, the previous example first compiles the pattern, which matches every word between the two *, and in addition to that it captures the word. Note that thanks to the ? metacharacter the pattern is non-greedy.

Note that \g<number> is there to avoid ambiguity with literal numbers, for example, imagine you need to add "1" right after a group:

```
>>> pattern = re.compile(r'\*(.*?)\*')
>>> pattern.sub(r"<b>\g<1>1<\\b>", text)
 'imagine→a→new→<b>world1<\\b>,→a→magic→<b>world1<\\b>'
```

As you can see, the behavior is as expected. Let's see what happens on using the notation without < and >:

```
>>> text = "imagine→a→new→*world*,→a→magic→*world*"
>>> pattern = re.compile(r'\*(.*?)\*')
>>> pattern.sub(r"<b>\g11<\\b>", text)
 error: bad group name
```

In the preceding example, the group is highlighted to remove ambiguity and help us see it, and that's precisely the problem the regex engine is facing. Here, the regex engine tries to use the group number 11 which doesn't exist. For this reason, there is the \g<group> notation.

Another thing to keep in mind with sub is that every backslash that escapes in the replacement string will be processed. As you can see in <\\b>, you need to escape them if you want to avoid it.

You can limit the number of replacements with the optional **count** argument.

subn(repl, string, count=0)

It is basically the same operation as sub, you can think of it as a utility above sub. It returns a tuple with the new string and the number of substitutions made. Let us see the working by using the same example as before:

```
>>> text = "imagine→a→new→*world*,→a→magic→*world*"
>>> pattern = re.compile(r'\*(.*?)\*')
>>> pattern.subn(r"<b>\g<1><\\b>", text)
 ('imagine→a→new→<b>world<\\b>,→a→magic→<b>world<\\b>', 2)
```

It's been a long section. We explored the main operations we can do with re module and the RegexObject class along with examples. Let's continue with the object we get after a match.

MatchObject

This object represents the matched pattern; you will get one every time you execute one of these operations:

- match
- search
- finditer

This object provides us with a set of operations for working with the captured groups, getting information about the position of the match, and so on. Let's see the most important operations.

group([group1, …])

The group operation gives you the subgroups of the match. If it's invoked with no arguments or zero, it will return the entire match; while if one or more group identifiers are passed, the corresponding groups' matches will be returned.

Let's see them with an example:

```
>>> pattern = re.compile(r"(\w+) (\w+)")
>>> match = pattern.search("Hello→world")
```

The pattern matches the whole string and captures two groups, Hello and world. Once we have the match, we can see the the following concrete cases:

- With no arguments or zero, it returns the entire match.
  ```
  >>> match.group()
  'Hello→world'
  ```

  ```
  >>> match.group(0)
  'Hello→world'
  ```

- With group1 bigger than 0, it returns the corresponding group.
  ```
  >>> match.group(1)
  'Hello'
  ```

  ```
  >>> match.group(2)
  'world'
  ```

- If the group doesn't exist, an IndexError will be thrown.
  ```
  >>> match.group(3)
  ...
  IndexError: no such group
  ```

- With multiple arguments, it returns the corresponding groups.

```
>>> match.group(0, 2)
    ('Hello→world', 'world')
```

In this case, we want the whole pattern and the second group, that's why we pass 0 and 2.

Groups can be named, we'll see it in depth in the next chapter; there is a special notation for it. If the pattern has named groups, they can be accessed using the names or the index:

```
>>> pattern = re.compile(r"(?P<first>\w+) (?P<second>\w+)")
```

In the preceding example, we've compiled a pattern to capture two groups: the first one is named first and the second one is named second.

```
>>> match = pattern.search("Hello→world")
>>> match.group('first')
'Hello'
```

In this way, we can get a group by its name. Note that using named groups we can still get the groups by their index, as shown in the following code:

```
>>> match.group(1)
'Hello'
```

We can even use both types:

```
>>> match.group(0, 'first', 2)
('Hello→world', 'Hello', 'world')
```

groups([default])

The groups operation is similar to the previous operation. However, in this case it returns a tuple with all the subgroups in the match instead of giving you one or some of the groups. Let's see it with the example we've used in the previous section:

```
>>> pattern = re.compile("(\w+) (\w+)")
>>> match = pattern.search("Hello→World")
>>> match.groups()
    ('Hello', 'World')
```

As we had in the previous section, we have two groups Hello and World and that's exactly what groups gives us. In this case, you can see groups as group(1, lastGroup).

In case there are groups that don't match, the default argument is returned.
If the default argument is not specified then None is used, for example:

```
>>> pattern = re.compile("(\w+) (\w+)?")
>>> match = pattern.search("Hello⋯→")
>>> match.groups("mundo")
   ('Hello', 'mundo')
>>> match.groups()
   ('Hello', None)
```

The pattern in the preceding example is trying to match two groups made of one or
more alphanumeric characters. The second one is optional; so we get only one group
with the string Hello. After getting the match, we call groups with default set to
mundo so that it returns mundo as the second group. Note that in the following call
we don't set default, so None is returned.

groupdict([default])

The groupdict method is used in the cases where named groups have been used.
It will return a dictionary with all the groups that were found:

```
>>> pattern = re.compile(r"(?P<first>\w+) (?P<second>\w+)")
>>> pattern.search("Hello⋯→world").groupdict()
{'first': 'Hello', 'second': 'world'}
```

In the preceding example, we use a pattern similar to what we've seen in the
previous sections. It captures two groups with the names first and second.
So, groupdict returns them in a dictionary. Note that if there aren't named
groups, then it returns an empty dictionary.

Don't worry if you don't understand quite well what is happening here. As we've
mentioned before, we'll see everything related to groups in *Chapter 3, Groups*.

start([group])

Sometimes, it is useful to know the index where the pattern matched. As with all the
operations related to groups, if the argument group is zero, then the operation works
with the whole string matched:

```
>>> pattern = re.compile(r"(?P<first>\w+) (?P<second>\w+)?")
>>> match = pattern.search("Hello⋯→")
>>> match.start(1)
0
```

If there are groups that don't match, then `-1` is returned:

```
>>> math = pattern.search("Hello⋯➔")
>>> match..start(2)
-1
```

end([group])

The `end` operation behaves exactly the same as `start`, except that it returns the end of the substring matched by the group:

```
>>> pattern = re.compile(r"(?P<first>\w+) (?P<second>\w+)?")
>>> match = pattern.search("Hello⋯➔")
>>> match.end (1)
5
```

span([group])

It's an operation that gives you a tuple with the values from `start` and `end`. This operation is often used in text editors to locate and highlight a search. The following code is an example of this operation:

```
>>> pattern = re.compile(r"(?P<first>\w+) (?P<second>\w+)?")
>>> match = pattern.search("Hello⋯➔")
>>> match.span(1)
(0, 5)
```

expand(template)

This operation returns the string after replacing it with backreferences in the template string. It's similar to `sub`.

Continuing with the example in the previous section:

```
>>> text = "imagine⋯➔a➔new⋯➔*world*,⋯➔a➔magic⋯➔*world*"
>>> match = re.search(r'\*(.*?)\*', text)
>>> match.expand(r"<b>\g<1><\\b>")
  '<b>world<\\b>'
```

Module operations

Let's see two useful operations from the module.

escape()

It escapes the literals that may appear in the expressions.

```
>>> re.findall(re.escape("^"), "^like^")
['^', '^']
```

purge()

It purges the regular expressions cache. We've already talked about this; you need to use this in order to release memory when you're using the operations through the module. Keep in mind that there is a tradeoff with the performance; once you release the cache, every pattern has to be compiled and cached again.

Well done, you already know the main operations that you can do with the `re` module. After this, you can start using regex in your projects without many problems.

Now, we're going to see how to change the default behavior of the patterns.

Compilation flags

When compiling a pattern string into a pattern object, it's possible to modify the standard behavior of the patterns. In order to do that, we have to use the compilation flags. These can be combined using the bitwise OR "`|`".

Flag	Python	Description
`re.IGNORECASE` or `re.I`	2.x 3.x	The pattern will match lower case and upper case.
`re.MULTILINE` or `re.M`	2.x 3.x	This flag changes the behavior of two metacharacters: • `^`: Which now matches at the beginning of the string and at the beginning of each new line. • `$`: In this case, it matches at the end of the string and the end of each line. Concretely, it matches right before the newline character.
`re.DOTALL` or `re.S`	2.x 3.x	The metacharacter "`.`" will match any character even the newline.

Flag	Python	Description
re.LOCALE or re.L	2.x 3.x	This flag makes \w, \W, \b, \B, \s, and \S dependent on the current locale.
		"re.LOCALE just passes the character to the underlying C library. It really only works on bytestrings which have 1 byte per character. UTF-8 encodes code points outside the ASCII range to multiple bytes per code point, and the re module will treat each of those bytes as a separate character." (at http://www.gossamer-threads.com/lists/python/python/850772)
		Note that when using re.L and re.U together (re.L|re.U, only Locale is used). Also, note that in Python 3 the use of this flag is discouraged; go to the documentation for more info.
re.VERBOSE or re.X	2.x 3.x	It allows writing of regular expressions that are easier to read and understand. For that, it treats some characters in a special way:
		• Whitespace is ignored except when it's in character class or preceded by a backslash
		• All characters to the right of the # are ignored like it was a comment, except when # is preceded by the backslash or it's in a character class.
re.DEBUG	2.x 3.x	It gives you information about the compilation pattern.
re.UNICODE or re.U	2.x	It makes \w, \W, \b, \B, \d, \D, \s, and \S dependent on the Unicode character properties database.
re.ASCII or re.A (only Python 3)	3.x	It makes \w, \W, \b, \B, \d, \D, \s, and \S perform ASCII-only matching. This makes sense because in Python 3 the matches are Unicode by default. You can find more on this in the *What's new on Python 3* section.

Let's see some examples of the most important flags.

re.IGNORECASE or re.I

As you can see, the following pattern matches even though the string starts with A and not with an a.

```
>>> pattern = re.compile(r"[a-z]+", re.I)
>>> pattern.search("Felix")
<_sre.SRE_Match at 0x10e27a238>
>>> pattern.search("felix")
<_sre.SRE_Match at 0x10e27a510>
```

re.MULTILINE or re.M

In the following example, the pattern doesn't match the date after newline because we're not using the flag:

```
>>> pattern = re.compile("^\w+\: (\w+/\w+/\w+)")
>>> pattern.findall("date: ⇢12/01/2013 \ndate: 11/01/2013")
['12/01/2013']
```

However, on using the `Multiline` flag, it matches the two dates:

```
>>> pattern = re.compile("^\w+\: (\w+/\w+/\w+)", re.M)
>>> pattern.findall("date: ⇢12/01/2013⇢\ndate: ⇢11/01/2013")
  ['12/01/2013', '12/01/2013']
```

 This is not the best way to capture a date.

re.DOTALL or re.S

Let's try to match anything after a digit:

```
>>> re.findall("^\d(.)", "1\ne")
  []
```

We can see in the previous example that the character class . with its default behavior doesn't match the newline. Let's see what happens on using the flag:

```
>>> re.findall("^\d(.)", "1\ne", re.S)
['\n']
```

As expected, on using the DOTALL flag it matches the newline perfectly.

re.LOCALE or re.L

In the following example, we get the first 256 characters and then we try to find every alphanumeric character in the string, so we obtain the expected characters as follows:

```
>>> chars = ''.join(chr(i) for i in xrange(256))
>>> " ".join(re.findall(r"\w", chars))
'0 1 2 3 4 5 6 7 8 9 A B C D E F G H I J K L M N O P Q R S T U V W X Y
Z _ a b c d e f g h i j k l m n o p q r s t u v w x y z'
```

After setting the locale to our system locale, we can again try to obtain every alphanumeric character:

```
>>> locale.setlocale(locale.LC_ALL, '')
'ru_RU.KOI8-R'
```

In this case, we get many more characters according to the new locale:

```
>>> " ".join(re.findall(r"\w", chars, re.LOCALE))
'0 1 2 3 4 5 6 7 8 9 A B C D E F G H I J K L M N O P Q R S T U V W X Y
Z _ a b c d e f g h i j k l m n o p q r s t u v w x y z \xa3 \xb3 \xc0
\xc1 \xc2 \xc3 \xc4 \xc5 \xc6 \xc7 \xc8 \xc9 \xca \xcb \xcc \xcd \xce
\xcf \xd0 \xd1 \xd2 \xd3 \xd4 \xd5 \xd6 \xd7 \xd8 \xd9 \xda \xdb \xdc
\xdd \xde \xdf \xe0 \xe1 \xe2 \xe3 \xe4 \xe5 \xe6 \xe7 \xe8 \xe9 \xea
\xeb \xec \xed \xee \xef \xf0 \xf1 \xf2 \xf3 \xf4 \xf5 \xf6 \xf7 \xf8
\xf9 \xfa \xfb \xfc \xfd \xfe \xff'
```

re.UNICODE or re.U

Let's try to find all the alphanumeric characters in a string:

```
>>> re.findall("\w+", "this→is→an→example")
['this', 'is', 'an', 'example']
```

But what would happen if we want to do the same with other languages? The alphanumeric characters depend on the language, so we need to indicate it to the regex engine:

```
>>> re.findall(ur"\w+", u"这是一个例子", re.UNICODE)
  [u'\u8fd9\u662f\u4e00\u4e2a\u4f8b\u5b50']
>>> re.findall(ur"\w+", u"مثال هذا", re.UNICODE)
  [u'\u0647\u0630\u0627', u'\u0645\u062b\u0627\u0644']
```

re.VERBOSE or re.X

In the following pattern, we've used several ···›; the first one is ignored because it is not in a character class or preceded by a backslash and the second one is part of the pattern. We've also used # three times, the first and the third one are ignored because they're not preceded by a backslash, and the second one is part of the pattern.

```
>>> pattern = re.compile(r"""[#|_] + #comment
              \ \# #comment
              \d+""", re.VERBOSE)
>>> pattern.findall("#···›#2")
['#···›#2']
```

re.DEBUG

```
>>>re.compile(r"[a-f|3-8]", re.DEBUG)
  in
    range (97, 102)
    literal 124
    range (51, 56)
```

Python and regex special considerations

In this section, we will review differences with other flavors, how to deal with Unicode, and also differences in the re module between Python 2.x and Python 3.

Differences between Python and other flavors

As we mentioned at the beginning of the book, the re module has Perl-style regular expressions. However, that doesn't mean Python support every feature the Perl engine has.

There are too many differences to cover them in a short book like this, if you want to know them in-depth here you have two good places to start:

- http://en.wikipedia.org/wiki/Comparison_of_regular_expression_engines
- http://www.regular-expressions.info/reference.html

Unicode

When you're using Python 2.x and you want to match Unicode, the regex has to be Unicode escape. For example:

```
>>> re.findall(r"\u03a9", u"adeΩa")
[]
>>> re.findall(ur"\u03a9", u"adeΩa")
[u'\u03a9']
```

Note that if you use Unicode characters but the type of the string you're using is not Unicode, python automatically encodes it using the default encoding. For example, in my case I have UTF-8:

```
>>> u"Ω".encode("utf-8")
'\xce\xa9'
>>> "Ω"
'\xce\xa9'
```

So, you have to be careful while mixing types:

```
>>> re.findall(r'Ω', "adeΩa")
['\xce\xa9']
```

Here, you're not matching Unicode but the characters in the default encoding:

```
>>> re.findall(r'\xce\xa9', "adeΩa")
['\xce\xa9']
```

So, if you use Unicode in any of them, you're pattern won't match anything:

```
>>> re.findall(r'Ω', u"adeΩa")
[]
```

On the other hand, you can use Unicode on both sides and it would match as expected:

```
>>> re.findall(ur'Ω', u"adeΩa")
    [u'\u03a9']
```

The `re` module doesn't do Unicode case folding, so case insensitive doesn't work on Unicode:

```
>>> re.findall(ur"ñ" ,ur"Ñ", re.I)
[]
```

What's new in Python 3

There are some changes in Python 3 that affect the regex behavior, and new features have been added to the `re` module. First, let's review how the string notation has changed.

Type	Prefixed	Description

String		They are string literals. They're Unicode. The backslash is necessary to escape meaningful characters.
		
		`>>>"España \n"`
		`'España \n'`

Raw string	`r` or `R`	They're equal to literal strings with the exception of the backslashes, which are treated as normal characters.
		
		`>>>r"España \n"`
		`'España \\n'`

Byte strings	`b` or `B`	Strings represented as bytes. They can only contain ASCII characters; if the byte is greater than 128, it must be escaped.
		
		`>>> b"Espa\xc3\xb1a \n"`
		`b'Espa\xc3\xb1a \n'`
		
		We can convert to Unicode in this way:
		
		`>>> str(b"Espa\xc3\xb1a \n", "utf-8")`
		`'España \n'`
		
		The backslash is necessary to escape meaningful characters.

Byte raw string	`r` or `R`	They are like byte strings, but the backslashes are escaped.
		
		`>>> br"Espa\xc3\xb1a \n"`
		`b'Espa\\xc3\\xb1a \\n'`
		
		So, the backslash used to escape bytes are escaped again, which complicates their conversion to Unicode:
		
		`>>> str(br"Espa\xc3\xb1a \n", "utf-8")`
		`'Espa\\xc3\\xb1a \\n'`

Unicode	`r` or `U`	The u prefix was removed in the early versions of Python 3, and recovered in version 3.3 the syntax is accepted again. They're equal to strings.

Literal strings are Unicode by default in Python 3, which means that there is no need to use the flag Unicode anymore.

```
>>> re.findall(r"\w+", "这是一个例子")
    ['这是一个例子']
```

Python 3.3 (http://docs.python.org/dev/whatsnew/3.3.html) adds more features related to Unicode and how it is treated in the language. For example, it adds support for the complete range of code points, including non-BMP (http://en.wikipedia.org/wiki/Plane_(Unicode)). So, for example:

- In Python 2.7:

```
>>> re.findall(r".", u'\U0010FFFF')
[u'\udbff', u'\udfff']
```

- In Python 3.3.2:

```
>>> re.findall(r".", u'\U0010FFFF')
['\U0010ffff']
```

As we've seen in the *Compilation Flags* section, the ASCII flag has been added.

Another important aspect to note when using Python 3 has to do with metacharacters. As the strings are Unicode by default, the metacharacters too, unless you use 8-bit patterns or use the ASCII flag.

```
>>> re.findall(r"\w+", "مثا اذه→ل")
['اذه', 'مثا ل']
>>> re.findall(r"\w+", "مثا اذه→ل word", re.ASCII)
['word']
```

In the preceding example, the characters that aren't ASCII are ignored.

Take into account that Unicode pattern and 8-bit patterns cannot be mixed.

In the following example, we've tried to match an 8-bit pattern against a Unicode String, that's why an exception is thrown (remember that it would work in Python 2.x):

```
>>> re.findall(b"\w+", b"hello⋯world")
[b'hello', b'world']
>>> re.findall(b"\w+", "hello world")
... .
TypeError: can't use a bytes pattern on a string-like object
```

Summary

This was a long chapter! We've covered a lot of material in it. We began with how strings work in Python and their different notations in Python 2.x and Python 3.x. After that, we looked at how to build regular expressions, the objects and interface the `re` module give us to deal with them, and the most important operations for searching and modifying strings. We also learned how to extract information from a pattern through `MatchObject`, such as the position or the groups of a match. We also learned how to modify the default behavior of some character classes and metacharacters using the compilation flags. And finally, we've seen how to deal with Unicode and the new features we can find in Python 3.x.

Throughout this chapter, we've seen that groups are crucial part of regular expressions and that many operations of the `re` module are meant to be used with groups. That's why we cover groups in depth in the following chapter.

3
Grouping

Grouping is a powerful tool that allows you to perform operations such as:

- Creating subexpressions to apply quantifiers. For instance, repeating a subexpression rather than a single character.

- Limiting the scope of the alternation. Instead of alternating the whole expression, we can define exactly what has to be alternated.

- Extracting information from the matched pattern. For example, extracting a date from lists of orders.

- Using the extracted information again in the regex, which is probably the most useful property. One example would be to detect repeated words.

Throughout this chapter, we will explore groups, from the simplest to the most complex ones. We'll review some of the previous examples in order to bring clarity to how these operations work.

Introduction

We've already used groups in several examples throughout *Chapter 2, Regular Expressions with Python*. Grouping is accomplished through two metacharacters, the parentheses (). The simplest example of the use of parentheses would be building a subexpression. For example, imagine you have a list of products, the ID for each product being made up of two or three sequences of one digit followed by a dash and followed by one alphanumeric character, 1-a2-b:

```
>>>re.match(r"(\d-\w){2,3}", ur"1-a2-b")
<_sre.SRE_Match at 0x10f690738>
```

As you can see in the preceding example, the parentheses indicate to the regex engine that the pattern inside them has to be treated like a unit.

Let's see another example; in this case, we need to match whenever there is one or more `ab` followed by `c`:

```
>>>re.search(r"(ab)+c", ur"ababc")
<_sre.SRE_Match at 0x10f690a08>
>>>re.search(r"(ab)+c", ur"abbc")
None
```

So, you could use parentheses whenever you want to group meaningful subpatterns inside the main pattern.

Another simple example of their use is limiting the scope of alternation. For example, let's say we would like to write an expression to match if someone is from Spain. In Spanish, the country is spelled España and Spaniard is spelled Español. So, we want to match España and Español. The Spanish letter ñ can be confusing for non-Spanish speakers, so in order to avoid confusion we'll use Espana and Espanol instead of España and Español.

We can achieve it with the following alternation:

```
>>>re.search("Espana|ol", "Espanol")
<_sre.SRE_Match at 0x1043cfe68>
>>>re.search("Espana|ol", "Espana")
<_sre.SRE_Match at 0x1043cfed0>
```

The problem is that this also matches `ol`:

```
>>>re.search("Espana|ol", "ol")
<_sre.SRE_Match at 0x1043cfe00>
```

So, let's try character classes as in the following code:

```
>>>re.search("Espan[aol]", "Espanol")
<_sre.SRE_Match at 0x1043cf1d0>

>>>re.search("Espan[aol]", "Espana")
<_sre.SRE_Match at 0x1043cf850>
```

It works, but here we have another problem: It also matches `"Espano"` and `"Espanl"` that doesn't mean anything in Spanish:

```
>>>re.search("Espan[a|ol]", "Espano")
<_sre.SRE_Match at 0x1043cfb28>
```

The solution here is to use parentheses:

```
>>>re.search("Espan(a|ol)", "Espana")
<_sre.SRE_Match at 0x10439b648>

>>>re.search("Espan(a|ol)", "Espanol")
<_sre.SRE_Match at 0x10439b918>

>>>re.search("Espan(a|ol)", "Espan")
    None

>>>re.search("Espan(a|ol)", "Espano")
    None

>>>re.search("Espan(a|ol)", "ol")
    None
```

Let's see another key feature of grouping, **capturing**. Groups also capture the matched pattern, so you can use them later in several operations, such as `sub` or in the regex itself.

For example, imagine you have a list of products, the IDs of which are made up of digits representing the country of the product, a dash as a separator, and one or more alphanumeric characters as the ID in the DB. You're requested to extract the country codes:

```
>>>pattern = re.compile(r"(\d+)-\w+")
>>>it = pattern.finditer(r"1-a\n20-baer\n34-afcr")
>>>match = it.next()
>>>match.group(1)
'1'
>>>match = it.next()
>>>match.group(1)
'20'
>>>match = it.next()
>>>match.group(1)
'34'
```

In the preceding example, we've created a pattern to match the IDs, but we're only capturing a group made up of the country digits. Remember that when working with the `group` method, the index 0 returns the whole match, and the groups start at index 1.

Capturing groups give a huge range of possibilities due to which they can also be used with several operations, which we would discuss in the upcoming sections.

Backreferences

As we've mentioned previously, one of the most powerful functionalities that grouping gives us is the possibility of using the captured group inside the regex or other operations. That's exactly what backreferences provide. Probably the best known example to bring some clarity is the regex to find duplicated words, as shown in the following code:

```
>>>pattern = re.compile(r"(\w+) \1")
>>>match = pattern.search(r"hello hello world")
>>>match.groups()
('hello',)
```

Here, we're capturing a group made up of one or more alphanumeric characters, after which the pattern tries to match a whitespace, and finally we have the \1 backreference. You can see it highlighted in the code, meaning that it must exactly match the same thing it matched as the first group.

Backreferences can be used with the first 99 groups .Obviously, with an increase in the number of groups, you will find the task of reading and maintaining the regex more complex. This is something that can be reduced with named groups; we'll see them in the following section. But before that, we still have a lot of things to learn with backreferences. So, let's continue with another operation in which backreferences really come in handy. Recall the previous example, in which we had a list of products. Now, let's try to change the order of the ID, so we have the ID in the DB, a dash, and the country code:

```
>>>pattern = re.compile(r"(\d+)-(\w+)")
>>>pattern.sub(r"\2-\1", "1-a\n20-baer\n34-afcr")
'a-1\nbaer-20\nafcr-34'
```

That's it. Easy, isn't it? Note that we're also capturing the ID in the DB, so we can use it later. With the highlighted code, we're saying, "Replace what you've matched with the second group, a dash, and the first group".

As with the previous example, using numbers can be difficult to follow and to maintain. So, let's see what Python, through the re module, offers to help with this.

Named groups

Remember from the previous chapter when we got a group through an index?

```
>>>pattern = re.compile(r"(\w+) (\w+)")
>>>match = pattern.search("Hello⇢world")
>>>match.group(1)
  'Hello'
>>>match.group(2)
  'world'
```

We just learnt how to access the groups using indexes to extract information and to use it as backreferences. Using numbers to refer to groups can be tedious and confusing, and the worst thing is that it doesn't allow you to give meaning or context to the group. That's why we have named groups.

Imagine a regex in which you have several backreferences, let's say 10, and you find out that the third one is invalid, so you remove it from the regex. That means you have to change the index for every backreference starting from that one onwards. In order to solve this problem, in 1997, Guido Van Rossum designed named groups for Python 1.5. This feature was offered to Perl for cross-pollination.

Nowadays, it can be found in almost any flavor. Basically it allows us to give names to the groups, so we can refer to them by their names in any operation where groups are involved.

In order to use it, we have to use the syntax, (?P<name>pattern), where the P comes from Python-specific extensions (as you can read in the e-mail Guido sent to Perl developers at http://markmail.org/message/oyezhwvefvotacc3)

Let's see how it works with the previous example in the following code snippet:

```
>>> pattern = re.compile(r"(?P<first>\w+) (?P<second>\w+)")
>>> match = re.search("Hello world")
>>>match.group("first")
  'Hello'
>>>match.group("second")
  'world'
```

So, backreferences are now much simpler to use and maintain as is evident in the following example:

```
>>>pattern = re.compile(r"(?P<country>\d+)-(?P<id>\w+)")
>>>pattern.sub(r"\g<id>-\g<country>", "1-a\n20-baer\n34-afcr")
'a-1\nbaer-20\nafcr-34'
```

As we see in the previous example, in order to reference a group by the name in the `sub` operation, we have to use `\g<name>`.

We can also use named groups inside the pattern itself, as seen in the following example:

```
>>>pattern = re.compile(r"(?P<word>\w+) (?P=word)")
>>>match = pattern.search(r"hello hello world")
>>>match.groups()
('hello',)
```

This is simpler and more readable than using numbers.

Through these examples, we've used the following three different ways to refer to named groups:

Use	Syntax
Inside a pattern	(?P=name)
In the `repl` string of the `sub` operation	\g<name>
In any of the operations of the `MatchObject`	match.group('name')

Non-capturing groups

As we've mentioned before, capturing content is not the only use of groups. There are cases when we want to use groups, but we're not interested in extracting the information; alternation would be a good example. That's why we have a way to create groups without capturing. Throughout this book, we've been using groups to create subexpressions, as can be seen in the following example:

```
>>>re.search("Españ(a|ol)", "Español")
<_sre.SRE_Match at 0x10e90b828>
>>>re.search("Españ(a|ol)", "Español").groups()
('ol',)
```

You can see that we've captured a group even though we're not interested in the content of the group. So, let's try it without capturing, but first we have to know the syntax, which is almost the same as in normal groups, `(?:pattern)`. As you can see, we've only added `?:`. Let's see the following example:

```
>>>re.search("Españ(?:a|ol)", "Español")
<_sre.SRE_Match at 0x10e912648>
>>>re.search("Españ(?:a|ol)", "Español").groups()
()
```

After using the new syntax, we have the same functionality as before, but now we're saving resources and the regex is easier to maintain. Note that the group cannot be referenced.

Atomic groups

They're a special case of non-capturing groups; they're usually used to improve performance. It disables backtracking, so with them you can avoid cases where trying every possibility or path in the pattern doesn't make sense. This concept is difficult to understand, so stay with me up to the end of the section.

The `re` module doesn't support atomic groups. So, in order to see an example, we're going to use the regex module: `https://pypi.python.org/pypi/regex`.

Imagine we have to look for an ID made up of one or more alphanumeric characters followed by a dash and by a digit:

```
>>>data = "aaaaabbbbbaaaacccccddddaaa"
>>>regex.match("(\w+)-\d",data)
```

Let's see step by step what's happening here:

1. The regex engine matches the first a.
2. It then matches every character up to the end of the string.
3. It fails because it doesn't find the dash.
4. So, the engine does backtracking and tries the same with the following a.
5. Start the same process again.

It tries this with every character. If you think about what we're doing, it doesn't make any sense to keep trying once you have failed the first time. And that's exactly what an atomic group is useful for. For example:

```
>>>regex.match("(?>\w+)-\d",data)
```

Here we've added ?>, which indicates an atomic group, so once the regex engine fails to match, it doesn't keep trying with every character in the data.

Special cases with groups

Python provides us with some forms of groups that can help us to modify the regular expressions or even to match a pattern only when a previous group exists in the match, such as an if statement.

Flags per group

There is a way to apply the flags we've seen in *Chapter 2, Regular Expressions with Python*, using a special form of grouping: (?iLmsux).

Letter	Flag
i	re.IGNORECASE
L	re.LOCALE
m	re.MULTILINE
s	re.DOTALL
u	re.UNICODE
x	re.VERBOSE

For example:

```
>>>re.findall(r"(?u)\w+",ur"ñ")
[u'\xf1']
```

The above example is the same as:

```
>>>re.findall(r"\w+",ur"ñ", re.U)
[u'\xf1']
```

We've seen what these examples do several times in the previous chapter.

Remember that a flag is applied to the whole expression.

yes-pattern|no-pattern

This is a very useful case of groups. It tries to match a pattern in case a previous one was found. On the other hand, it doesn't try to match a pattern in case a previous group was not found. In short, it's like an if-else statement. The syntax for this operation is as follows:

```
(?(id/name)yes-pattern|no-pattern)
```

This expression means: if the group with this ID has already been matched, then at this point of the string, the `yes-pattern` pattern has to match. If the group hasn't been matched, then the `no-pattern` pattern has to match.

Let's see how it works continuing with our trite example. We have a list of products, but in this case the ID can be made in two different ways:

- The country code (two digits), a dash, three or four alphanumeric characters, a dash, and the area code (2 digits). For example: `34-adrl-01`.

- Three or four alphanumeric characters. For example: `adrl`.

So, when there is a country code, we need to match the country area:

```
>>>pattern = re.compile(r"(\d\d-)?(\w{3,4})(?(1)(-\d\d))")
>>>pattern.match("34-erte-22")
<_sre.SRE_Match at 0x10f68b7a0>
>>>pattern.search("erte")
<_sre.SRE_Match at 0x10f68b828>
```

As you can see in the previous example, there is a match when we have a country code and area code. Note that when there is a country code but no area code, there is no match:

```
>>>pattern.match("34-erte")
None
```

And what's `no-pattern` for? Let's add another constraint to the previous example: if there is no country code there has to be a name at the end of the string:

- The country code (2 digits), a dash, three or four alphanumeric characters, a dash, and the area code (2 digits). For example: `34-adrl-01`

- Three or four alphanumeric characters, followed by three or four characters. For example: `adrl-sala`.

Let's see it in action:

```
>>>pattern = re.compile(r"(\d\d-)?(\w{3,4})-(?(1)(\d\d)|[a-z]{3,4})$")
>>>pattern.match("34-erte-22")
<_sre.SRE_Match at 0x10f6ee750>
```

As expected, if there is a country code and an area code, there is a match.

```
>>>pattern.match("34-erte")
None
```

In the preceding example, we do have a country area, but there is no area code, so there is no match.

```
>>>pattern.match("erte-abcd")
<_sre.SRE_Match at 0x10f6ee880>
```

And finally, when there is no country area, there must be a name, so we have a match.

Note that `no-pattern` is optional, so in the first example, we've omitted it.

Overlapping groups

Throughout *Chapter 2, Regular Expressions with Python*, we've seen several operations where there was a warning about overlapping groups: for example, the `findall` operation. This is something that seems to confuse a lot of people. So, let's try to bring some clarity with a simple example:

```
>>>re.findall(r'(a|b)+', 'abaca')
['a', 'a']
```

What's happening here? Why does the following expression give us `'a'` and `'a'` instead of `'aba'` and `'a'`?

Let's look at it step by step to understand the solution:

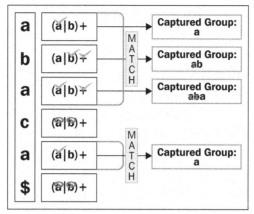

Overlapping groups matching process

As we can see in the preceding figure, the characters aba are matched, but the captured group is only formed by a. This is because even though our regex is grouping every character, it stays with the last a. Keep this in mind because it's the key to understanding how it works. Stop for a moment and think about it, we're requesting the regex engine to capture all the groups made up of a or b, but just for one of the characters and that's the key. So, how can you capture the groups made of several 'a' or 'b' in any order? The following expression does the trick:

```
>>>re.findall(r'((?:a|b)+)', 'abbaca')
    ['abba', 'a']
```

We're asking the regex engine to capture every group made up of the subexpression (a|b) and not to group just one character.

One last thing on this— if we would want to obtain every group made of a or b with findall, we could write this simple expression:

```
>>>re.findall(r'(a|b)', 'abaca')
    ['a', 'b', 'a', 'a']
```

In this case, we're asking the regex engine to capture a group made of a or b. As we're using findall, we get every pattern matched, so we get four groups.

> **Rule of Thumb**
>
> It's better to keep regular expressions as simple as you can. So, you should begin with the simplest expression and then build more complex expressions step by step and not the other way around.

Summary

Don't allow the simplicity of the chapter to fool you, what we have learned throughout this chapter will be very useful in your day-to-day work with regex, and it'll give you a lot of leverage.

Let's summarize what we have learned so far. First, we have seen how a group can help us when we need to apply quantifiers to only some part of the expression.

We have also learned how to use the captured groups in the pattern again or even in the replacement string in the sub operation, thanks to **backreferences**.

In this chapter, we have also viewed named groups, a tool for improving the readability and future maintenance of the regex.

Later on, we have learned to match a subexpression just in case a previous group exists or on the other hand, to match it when a previous group doesn't exist.

Now that we know how to use groups, it's time to learn a more complex subject very close to groups; look around!

4
Look Around

Until this point, we have learned different mechanisms of matching characters while discarding them. A character that is already matched cannot be compared again, and the only way to match any upcoming character is by discarding it.

The exceptions to this are a number of metacharacters we have studied, the so-called **zero-width assertions**. These characters indicate positions rather than actual content. For instance, the caret symbol (^) is a representation of the beginning of a line or the dollar sign ($) for the end of a line. They just ensure that the position in the input is correct without actually consuming or matching any character.

A more powerful kind of zero-width assertion is **look around**, a mechanism with which it is possible to match a certain previous (**look behind**) or ulterior (**look ahead**) value to the current position. They effectively do assertion without consuming characters; they just return a positive or negative result of the match.

The look around mechanism is probably the most unknown and at the same time the most powerful technique in regular expressions. This mechanism allows us to create powerful regular expressions that cannot be written otherwise, either because of the complexity it would represent or just because of technical limitations of regular expressions without look around.

In this chapter, we are going to learn how to leverage the look around mechanism using Python regular expressions. We will understand how to apply them, how these work behind the scenes, and the few limitations the Python regular expression module will impose on us.

Both look ahead and look behind could be subdivided into another two types each: positive and negative:

- **Positive look ahead**: This mechanism is represented as an expression preceded by a question mark and an equals sign, `?=`, inside a parenthesis block. For example, `(?=regex)` will match if the passed regex *do* match against the forthcoming input.

- **Negative look ahead**: This mechanism is specified as an expression preceded by a question mark and an exclamation mark, `?!`, inside a parenthesis block. For example, `(?!regex)` will match if the passed regex *do not* match against the forthcoming input.

- **Positive look behind**: This mechanism is represented as an expression preceded by a question mark, a less-than sign, and an equals sign, `?<=`, inside a parenthesis block. For example, `(?<=regex)` will match if the passed regex *do* match against the previous input.

- **Negative look behind**: This mechanism is represented as an expression preceded by a question mark, a less-than sign, and an exclamation mark, `?<!`, inside a parenthesis block. For example, `(?<!regex)` will match if the passed regex *do not* match against the previous input.

Let's start looking forward to the next section.

Look ahead

The first type of look around mechanism that we are going to study is the look ahead mechanism. It tries to match ahead the subexpression passed as an argument. The zero-width nature of the two look around operations render them complex and difficult to understand.

As we know from the previous section, it is represented as an expression preceded by a question mark and an equals sign, `?=`, inside a parenthesis block: `(?=regex)`.

Let's start tackling this by comparing the result of the two similar regular expressions. We can recall that in *Chapter 1*, *Introducing Regular Expressions*, we matched the expression `/fox/` to the phrase The quick brown fox jumps over the lazy dog. Let's also apply the expression `/(?=fox)/` to the same input:

```
>>>pattern = re.compile(r'fox')
>>>result = pattern.search("The quick brown fox jumps over the
lazy dog")
>>>print result.start(), result.end()
16 19
```

We just searched the literal `fox` in the input string, and just as expected we have found it between the index `16` and `19`. Let's see the following example of the look ahead mechanism:

```
>>>pattern = re.compile(r'(?=fox)')
>>>result = pattern.search("The quick brown fox jumps over the lazy
dog")
>>>print result.start(), result.end()
16 16
```

This time we have applied the expression `/(?=fox)/` instead. The result has been just a position at the index `16` (both the start and end point to the same index). This is because look around does not consume characters, and therefore, it can be used to filter where the expression should match. However, it will not define the contents of the result. We can visually compare these two expressions in the following figure:

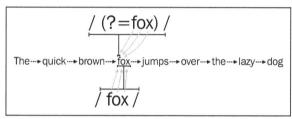

Comparison of normal and look ahead matches

Let's use this feature again to try and match any word that is followed by a comma character (`,`) using the following regular expression `/\w+(?=,)/` and the text `They were three: Felix, Victor, and Carlos`:

```
>>>pattern = re.compile(r'\w+(?=,)')
>>>pattern.findall("They were three: Felix, Victor, and Carlos.")
['Felix', 'Victor']
```

We created a regular expression that accepts any repetition of alphanumeric characters followed by a comma character that is not going to be used as a part of the result. Therefore, only `Felix` and `Victor` were part of the result as `Carlos` didn't have a comma after the name.

How different was this compared to the use of the regular expressions we have up to this chapter? Let's compare the results by applying `/\w+,/` to the same text:

```
>>>pattern = re.compile(r'\w+,')
>>>pattern.findall("They were three: Felix, Victor, and Carlos.")
['Felix,', 'Victor,']
```

With the preceding regular expressions, we asked the regular expression engine to accept any repetition of alphanumeric characters followed by a comma character. Therefore, the alphanumeric characters *and the comma character* will be returned, as we can see in the listing.

It's noteworthy that the look ahead mechanism is another subexpression that can be leveraged with all the power of regular expressions (it's not the same case for the look behind mechanism as we will discover later). Therefore, we can use all the constructions we learned so far as the alternation:

```
>>>pattern = re.compile(r'\w+(?=,|\.)')
>>>pattern.findall("They were three: Felix, Victor, and Carlos.")
['Felix', 'Victor', 'Carlos']
```

In the preceding example, we used alternation (even though we could have used other simpler techniques as a character set) to accept any repetition of alphanumeric characters followed by a comma or dot character that is not going to be used as a part of the result.

Negative look ahead

The negative look ahead mechanism presents the same nature of the look ahead but with a notable distinction: the result will be valid only if the subexpression doesn't match.

It is represented as an expression preceded by a question mark and an exclamation mark, ?!, inside a parenthesis block: (?!regex).

This is useful when we want to express what should not happen. For instance, to find any name John that is not John Smith, we could do the following:

```
>>>pattern = re.compile(r'John(?!\sSmith)')
>>> result = pattern.finditer("I would rather go out with John McLane
than with John Smith or John Bon Jovi")
>>>for i in result:
...print i.start(), i.end()
...
27 31
63 67
```

In the preceding example, we looked for John by consuming these five characters and then looked ahead for a whitespace character followed by the word Smith. In case of a match, the match will contain only the starting and end position of John. In this case, the positions are 27-31 for John McLane and 63-67 for John Bon Jovi.

Now, we are able to leverage the more basic forms of look around: the positive and negative look ahead. Let's learn how to get the most of it in substitutions and groups.

Look around and substitutions

The zero-width nature of the look around operation is especially useful in substitutions. Thanks to them, we are able to perform transformations that would otherwise be extremely complex to read and write.

One typical example of look ahead and substitutions would be the conversion of a number composed of just numeric characters, such as 1234567890, into a comma separated number, that is, 1,234,567,890.

In order to write this regular expression, we will need a strategy to follow. What we want to do is group the numbers in blocks of three that will then be substituted by the same group plus a comma character.

We can easily start with an almost naive approach with the following highlighted regular expression:

```
>>>pattern = re.compile(r'\d{1,3}')
>>>pattern.findall("The number is: 12345567890")
['123', '455', '678', '90']
```

We have failed in this attempt. We are effectively grouping in blocks of three numbers, but they should be taken from the right to the left. We need a different approach. Let's try to find one, two, or three digits that have to be followed by any number of blocks of three digits until we find something that is not a digit.

This will have the following effect on our number. When trying to find one, two, or three digits, the regular expression will start taking just one, and this will be the number 1. Then, it will try to catch blocks of exactly three numbers, for example, 234, 567, 890, until it finds a non-digit. This is the end of the input.

If we express in a regular expression what we have just explained in plain English, we will obtain the following:

```
/\d{1,3}(?=(\d{3})+(?!\d))/
```

Element	Description
\d	This matches a decimal character
{1,3}	This indicates that the match is repeated between one and three times
(?=	This indicates that the character is followed by (but not consuming) this expression
(	This indicates a group
\d	This indicates that there is a group of decimal characters
\s	This indicates that the match is repeated three times
)	
+	This indicates that the decimal character should appear one or more times
(?!	This indicates that the match is not followed by (but not consuming) what the following expression defines
\d	This indicates a decimal character
))	

Let's try again with this new regular expression in Python's console:

```
>>>pattern = re.compile(r'\d{1,3}(?=(\d{3})+(?!\d))')
>>>results = pattern.finditer('1234567890')
>>>for result in results:
...     print result.start(), result.end()
...
...
0 1
1 4
4 7
```

This time, we can see that we are using the right approach as we have just identified the correct blocks: 1, 234, 567, and 890.

Now, we just need to use a substitution to substitute each of the matches we have found for the same match result plus a comma character. We already know how to use substitutions as we learned it in *Chapter 2, Regular Expressions with Python,* so let's just put it into practice:

```
>>>pattern = re.compile(r'\d{1,3}(?=(\d{3})+(?!\d))')
>>>pattern.sub(r'\g<0>,', "1234567890")
'1,234,567,890'
```

Et voila! We have just transformed an unformatted number into a beautiful number with a thousand separators.

We have just learned the two techniques to look ahead and foresee what is coming. We have also studied their usage in substitutions. Now, let's turn our head back to see what we have left behind **look behind**.

Look behind

We could safely define look behind as the opposite operation to look ahead. It tries to match behind the subexpression passed as an argument. It has a zero-width nature as well, and therefore, it won't be part of the result.

It is represented as an expression preceded by a question mark, a less-than sign, and an equals sign, ?<=, inside a parenthesis block: (?<=regex).

We could, for instance, use it in an example similar to the one we used in negative look ahead to find just the surname of someone named John McLane. To accomplish this, we could write a look behind like the following:

```
>>>pattern = re.compile(r'(?<=John\s)McLane')
>>>result = pattern.finditer("I would rather go out with John McLane
than with John Smith or John Bon Jovi")
>>>for i in result:
...    print i.start(), i.end()
...
32 38
```

With the preceding look behind, we requested the regex engine to match only positions that are preceded with John and a whitespace to then consume McLane as a result.

In Python's `re` module, there is, however, a fundamental difference between how look ahead and look behind are implemented. Due to a number of deeply rooted technical reasons, the look behind mechanism is only able to match fixed-width patterns. If variable-width patterns in look behind are required, the regex module at `https://pypi.python.org/pypi/regex` can be leveraged instead of the standard Python `re` module.

Fixed-width patterns don't contain variable-length matchers such as the quantifiers we studied in *Chapter 1, Introducing Regular Expressions*. Other variable-length constructions such as back references aren't allowed either. Alternation is allowed but only if the alternatives have the same length. Again, these limitations are not present in the aforementioned regex module.

Let's see what'll happen if we use an alternation with different length alternatives in a back reference:

```
>>>pattern = re.compile(r'(?<=(John|Jonathan)\s)McLane')
Traceback (most recent call last):
  File "<stdin>", line 1, in <module>
  File "/System/Library/Frameworks/Python.framework/Versions/2.7/lib/
python2.7/re.py", line 190, in compile
return _compile(pattern, flags)
  File "/System/Library/Frameworks/Python.framework/Versions/2.7/lib/
python2.7/re.py", line 242, in _compile
raise error, v # invalid expression
sre_constants.error: look-behind requires fixed-width pattern
```

We've got an exception as look behind requires a fixed-width pattern. We will get a similar result if we try to apply quantifiers or other variable-length constructions.

Now that we have learned different techniques to match ahead or behind without consuming characters and the different limitations we might have, we can try to write another example that embraces a few of the mechanisms that we have studied to solve a real-world problem.

Let's assume that we want to extract any Twitter username that is present in a tweet in order to create an automatic mood detection system. To write a regular expression in order to extract them, we should start by identifying how a Twitter username is represented. If we browse the Twitter's site `https://support.twitter.com/articles/101299-why-can-t-i-register-certain-usernames`, we might find the following description:

> *"A username can only contain alphanumeric characters (letters A-Z, numbers 0-9) with the exception of underscores, as noted above. Check to make sure your desired username doesn't contain any symbols, dashes, or spaces."*

For our development tests, we are going to use this Packt Publishing tweet:

The first thing we should be able to construct is a character set with all the characters that could potentially be used in a Twitter username. This could be any alphanumeric character followed by the underscore character as we just found in the previous Twitter support article. Therefore, we could construct a character set similar to the following:

```
[\w_]
```

This will represent all the parts that we want to extract from the username. Then, we will need to prepend a word boundary and the at symbol (@) that will be used to locate the usernames:

```
/\B@[\w_]+/
```

The reason behind using the word boundary is that we don't want to get confused with e-mails and so on. We are looking only for text that follows the start of the line or a word boundary, then followed by an @ symbol, and then just a number of alphanumeric or underscore characters. The examples are as follows:

- @vromer0 is a valid user name

- iam@vromer0 is not a valid user name as it should start with the @ symbol

- @vromero.org is not a valid username as it contains an invalid character

If we use the regular expression we have at the moment, we will obtain the following result:

```
>>>pattern = re.compile(r'\B@[\w_]+')
>>>pattern.findall("Know your Big Data = 5 for $50 on eBooks and 40%
off all eBooks until Friday #bigdata #hadoop @HadoopNews packtpub.com/
bigdataoffers")
['@HadoopNews']
```

We do want to match just the username without including the preceding @ symbol. At this point, a look behind mechanism becomes useful. We can include the word boundary and the @ symbol in a look behind subexpression so that they don't become a part of the matched result:

```
>>>pattern = re.compile(r'(?<=\B@)[\w_]+')
>>>pattern.findall("Know your Big Data = 5 for $50 on eBooks and 40%
off all eBooks until Friday #bigdata #hadoop @HadoopNews packtpub.com/
bigdataoffers")
['HadoopNews']
```

And now we have accomplished our goals.

Negative look behind

The negative look behind mechanism presents the very same nature of the main look behind mechanism, but we will only have a valid result if the passed subexpression doesn't match.

It is represented as an expression preceded by a question mark, a less-than sign, and an exclamation mark, `?<!`, inside a parenthesis block: `(?<!regex)`.

It is worth remembering that negative look behind not only shares most of the characteristics of the look behind mechanism, but it also shares the limitations. The negative look behind mechanism is only able to match fixed-width patterns. These have the same cause and implications as we have studied in the previous section.

We could put this into practice by trying to match any person surnamed `Doe` who is not named `John` with a regular expression like this: `/(?<!John\s)Doe/`. If we use it in Python's console, we will obtain the following result:

```
>>>pattern = re.compile(r'(?<!John\s)Doe')
>>>results = pattern.finditer("John Doe, Calvin Doe, Hobbes Doe")
>>>for result in results:
...    print result.start(), result.end()
...
17 20
29 32
```

Look around and groups

Another beneficial use of look around constructions is inside groups. Typically, when groups are used, a very specific result has to be matched and returned inside the group. As we don't want to pollute the groups with information that is not required, among other potential options we can leverage look around as a favorable solution.

Let's say that we need to get a comma-separated value, the first part of the value is a name, while the second is a value. The format would be similar to this:

```
INFO 2013-09-17 12:13:44,487 authentication failed
```

As we learned in *Chapter 3*, *Grouping*, we can easily write an expression that will get these two values like the following:

```
/\w+\s[\d-]+\s[\d:,]+\s(.*\sfailed)/
```

However, we only want to match when the failure is not an authentication failure. We can accomplish this with the addition of a negative look behind. It will look like this:

```
/\w+\s[\d-]+\s[\d:,]+\s(.*(?<!authentication\s)failed)/
```

Once we put this in Python's console, we will get the following output:

```
>>>pattern = re.compile(r'\w+\s[\d-]+\s[\d:,]+\
s(.*(?<!authentication\s)failed)')
>>>pattern.findall("INFO 2013-09-17 12:13:44,487 authentication
failed")
[]
>>>pattern.findall("INFO 2013-09-17 12:13:44,487 something else
failed")
['something else failed']
```

Summary

In this chapter, we learned the concept of zero-with assertions and how it can be useful to find the exact thing in a text without interfering in the result content.

We have also learned how to leverage the four types of look around mechanisms: positive look ahead, negative look ahead, positive look behind, and negative look behind.

We also reviewed, with special interest, the limitation of the two types of look behind with the variable assertions.

With this, we conclude the travel through the basic and advanced techniques around regular expressions. Now, we are ready to focus on performance tuning in the next chapter.

5
Performance of Regular Expressions

Up to this point, we worried about learning how to leverage a feature or obtain a result without caring too much about how fast the process would be. Our only goals were correctness and readability.

In this chapter, we are going to steer towards a completely different concern—performance. However, we will find that often an improvement in performance will result in degradation of readability. When we are modifying something to make it faster, we are probably making it easier for the machine to understand, and therefore, we are probably compromising on human readability.

On December 4, 1974, Donald Knuth, the author of the famous book *The Art of Computer Programming*, wrote the paper *Structured Programming* with `go-to` statements. This well-known quote is extracted from the paper:

> "*Programmers waste enormous amounts of time thinking about, or worrying about, the speed of noncritical parts of their programs, and these attempts at efficiency actually have a strong negative impact when debugging and maintenance are considered. We should forget about small efficiencies, say about 97% of the time: premature optimization is the root of all evil. Yet we should not pass up our opportunities in that critical 3%.*"

That said, we should be careful about what we optimize. Probably, for a regular expression used to validate an e-mail address of a form, we should have more interest in readability than in performance. On the other hand, if we are writing a regular expression to be used in batch processing of huge historical files, we should be more interested in the performance.

The most commonly used approach for optimization is to first write, then measure, and only then optimize that critical 3 percent. So, in this chapter, first we are going to learn how to measure and analyze the regular expressions, and then follow on with optimization techniques.

Benchmarking regular expressions with Python

In order to benchmark our regex, we're going to measure the time a regex takes to execute. It's important to test them with different inputs, because with small inputs almost every regex is fast enough. However, with longer ones it can be a completely different beast, as we will see later in the section *Backtracking*.

First, we're going to create a small function to help us with this task:

```
>>> from time import clock as now
>>> def test(f, *args, **kargs):
        start = now()
        f(*args, **kargs)
        print "The function %s lasted: %f" %(f.__name__, now() -
start)
```

So, we can test a regex using the following code:

```
>>> def alternation(text):
        pat = re.compile('spa(in|niard)')
        pat.search(text)
>>> test(alternation, "spain")
The function alternation lasted: 0.000009
```

Python comes with a built-in profiler http://docs.python.org/2/library/profile.html that we can also use to measure the time and the number of calls, among other things:

```
>>> import cProfile
>>> cProfile.run("alternation('spaniard')")
```

You can see the output in the following screenshot:

```
In [45]: cProfile.run("re.search('(a+)+c', 'aaaaaaaaaaaaaaaaaaaa')")
         6 function calls in 0.145 seconds

   Ordered by: standard name

   ncalls  tottime  percall  cumtime  percall filename:lineno(function)
        1    0.000    0.000    0.145    0.145 <string>:1(<module>)
        1    0.000    0.000    0.145    0.145 re.py:145(search)
        1    0.000    0.000    0.000    0.000 re.py:232(_compile)
        1    0.000    0.000    0.000    0.000 {method 'disable' of '_lsprof.Profiler' objects}
        1    0.000    0.000    0.000    0.000 {method 'get' of 'dict' objects}
        1    0.145    0.145    0.145    0.145 {method 'search' of '_sre.SRE_Pattern' objects}
```

Profiling output

Let's see another useful technique that is going to help when you want to see what's going on under the hook of your regex. It's something that we've seen before in *Chapter 2, Regular Expressions with Python*, the flag DEBUG. Recall that it gives us information about how the pattern is compiled. For example:

```
>>> re.compile('(\w+\d+)+-\d\d', re.DEBUG)
max_repeat 1 4294967295
  subpattern 1
    max_repeat 1 4294967295
      in
        category category_word
    max_repeat 1 4294967295
      in
        category category_digit
literal 45
in
  category category_digit
in
  category category_digit
```

Here, we can see three `max_repeat` conditions from 1 to `4294967295`, two of them inside another `max_repeat`. Think about them as nested loops, as you're probably thinking this is a bad smell. In fact, this will lead you to a **catastrophic backtracking**, something that we'll see later.

The RegexBuddy tool

Among the different tools available for better productivity while writing regular expressions, **RegexBuddy** (http://www.regexbuddy.com/) by Just Great Software Co. Ltd. is outstanding.

The mastermind behind Just Great Software is Jan Goyvaerts, the same person who is behind **Regular-Expressions.info** (http://www.regular-expressions.info/), one of the most well-known references on the Internet for regular expressions.

With RegexBuddy, we can use a visual interface for building, testing, and debugging regular expressions. The debug feature is almost unique, and provides a great mechanism to understand how the regular expression engine is working behind the scenes. In the following screenshot, we can see RegexBuddy debugging the execution of a regular expression:

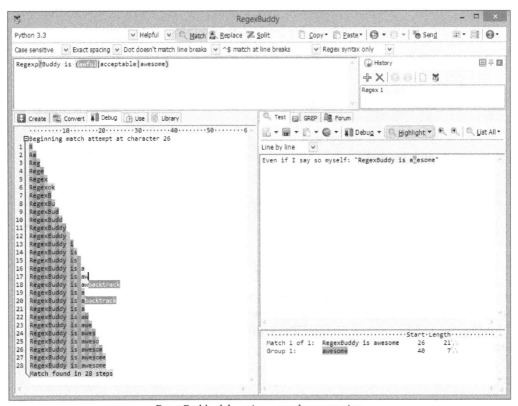

RegexBuddy debugging a regular expression

It does have other features, such as a library of commonly used regular expressions and a code generator for different programming environments.

Although it has a couple of downsides, its license is proprietary and the only build available is for Windows. However, the execution on Linux using the **wine emulator** is supported.

Understanding the Python regex engine

The `re` module uses a backtracking regular expression engine; although, in the very well-known book *Mastering Regular Expressions* by *Jeffrey E. F. Friedl*, it is classified as **Nondeterministic Finite Automata (NFA)** type. Also, according to *Tim Peters* (`https://mail.python.org/pipermail/tutor/2006-January/044335.html`), the module is not purely NFA.

These are the most common characteristics of the algorithm:

- It supports "lazy quantifiers" such as `*?`, `+?`, and `??`.
- It matches the first coincidence, even though there are longer ones in the string.

  ```
  >>>re.search("engineer|engineering", "engineering").group()
  'engineer'
  ```

  This also means that order is important.

- The algorithm tracks only one transition at one step, which means that the engine checks one character at a time.
- Backreferences and capturing parentheses are supported.
- **Backtracking** is the ability to remember the last successful position so that it can go back and retry if needed
- In the worst case, complexity is exponential $O(c^n)$. We'll see this later in *Backtracking*.

Backtracking

As we've mentioned before, backtracking allows going back and repeating the different paths of the regular expression. It does so by remembering the last successful position. This applies to alternation and quantifiers. Let's see an example:

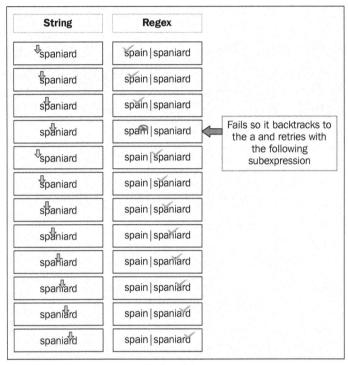

String	Regex
spaniard	spain|spaniard
spaniard	spain|spaniard
spaniard	spain|spaniard
spaniard	spain|spaniard
spaniard	spain|spaniard
spaniard	spain|spaniard
spaniard	spain|spaniard
spaniard	spain|spaniard
spaniard	spain|spaniard
spaniard	spain|spaniard
spaniard	spain|spaniard
spaniard	spain|spaniard

Fails so it backtracks to the a and retries with the following subexpression

Backtracking

As you can see in the preceding figure, the regex engine tries to match one character at a time until it fails, and then starts again with the next path it can retry.

The regex used in the figure is a perfect example of the importance of how the regex is built. In this case, the expression can be rebuilt as `spa(in|niard)` so that the regex engine doesn't have to go back to the start of the string in order to retry the second alternative.

This leads us to something called a catastrophic backtracking; a well-known problem with backtracking that can give you several problems ranging from slow regex to a crash with a stack overflow.

In the previous example, you can see that the behavior grows not only with the input but also with different paths in the regex, so the algorithm can be exponential O(c^n). With this in mind, it's easy to understand why we can end up with a stack overflow. The problem arises when the regex fails to match the string. Let's benchmark a regex with a technique we've seen previously so that we can understand the problem better.

First, let's try a simple regex:

```
>>> def catastrophic(n):
        print "Testing with %d characters" %n
        pat = re.compile('(a+)+c')
text = "%s" %('a' * n)
        pat.search(text)
```

As you can see, the text we're trying to match is always going to fail as there is no c at the end. Let's test it with different inputs:

```
>>> for n in range(20, 30):
        test(catastrophic, n)
Testing with 20 characters
The function catastrophic lasted: 0.130457
Testing with 21 characters
The function catastrophic lasted: 0.245125
......
The function catastrophic lasted: 14.828221
Testing with 28 characters
The function catastrophic lasted: 29.830929
Testing with 29 characters
The function catastrophic lasted: 61.110949
```

The behavior of this regex looks as if it is quadratic. But why? What's happening here? The problem is that (a+) starts greedy, so it tries to get as many a characters as possible. After that, it fails to match the c, that is, it backtracks to the second a, and continues consuming a characters until it fails to match c. And then, it tries the whole process again (backtracks) starting with the second a character.

Let's see another example, in this case with an exponential behavior:

```
>>> def catastrophic(n):
        print "Testing with %d characters" %n
        pat = re.compile('(x+)+(b+)+c')
        text = 'x' * n
        text += 'b' * n
```

```
        pat.search(text)
>>> for n in range(12, 18):
        test(catastrophic, n)
Testing with 12 characters
The function catastrophic lasted: 1.035162
Testing with 13 characters
The function catastrophic lasted: 4.084714
Testing with 14 characters
The function catastrophic lasted: 16.319145
Testing with 15 characters
The function catastrophic lasted: 65.855182
Testing with 16 characters
The function catastrophic lasted: 276.941307
```

As you can see, the behavior is exponential, which can lead to catastrophic scenarios. Finally, let's see what happens when the regex has a match:

```
>>> def non_catastrophic(n):
        print "Testing with %d characters" %n
        pat = re.compile('(x+)+(b+)+c')
        text = 'x' * n
        text += 'b' * n
        text += 'c'
        pat.search(text)
>>> for n in range(12, 18):
        test(non_catastrophic, n)
Testing with 10 characters
The function catastrophic lasted: 0.000029
......
Testing with 19 characters
The function catastrophic lasted: 0.000012
```

Optimization recommendations

In the following sections, we will find a number of recommendations that could be applied to improve regular expressions.

The best tool will always be common sense, and common sense will need to be used even while following these recommendations. It has to be understood when the recommendation is applicable and when it is not. For instance, the recommendation **don't be greedy** cannot be used in all the cases.

Reuse compiled patterns

We have learned in *Chapter 2, Regular Expressions with Python*, that to use a regular expression we have to convert it from its string representation to a compiled form as RegexObject.

This compilation takes some time. If we are using the rest of the module operations instead of using the compile function to avoid the creation of the RegexObject, we should understand that the compilation is executed anyway and a number of compiled RegexObject are cached automatically.

However, when we are compiling, that cache won't back us. Every single compile execution will consume an amount of time that perhaps could be negligible for a single execution, but it's definitely relevant if many executions are performed.

Let's see the difference between reusing and not reusing the compiled patterns in the following example:

```
>>> def dontreuse():
        pattern = re.compile(r'\bfoo\b')
        pattern.match("foo bar")

>>> def callonethousandtimes():
        for _ in range(1000):
            dontreuse()

>>> test(callonethousandtimes)
The function callonethousandtimes lasted: 0.001965

>>> pattern = re.compile(r'\bfoo\b')
>>> def reuse():
        pattern.match("foo bar")

>>> def callonethousandtimes():
        for _ in range(1000):
            reuse()

>>> test(callonethousandtimes)
The function callonethousandtimes lasted: 0.000633
>>>
```

Extract common parts in alternation

Alternation is always a performance risk in regular expressions. When using them in a sort of NFA implementation, in Python, we should extract any common part outside of the alternation.

For instance, if we have /(Hello⋯▸World|Hello⋯▸Continent|Hello⋯▸Country,)/, we could easily extract Hello⋯▸ with the following expression: /Hello⋯▸(World|Continent|Country)/. This would enable our engine to just check Hello⋯▸ once, and it will not go back to recheck for each possibility. In the following example, we can see the difference on execution:

```
>>> pattern = re.compile(r'/(Hello\sWorld|Hello\sContinent|Hello\
sCountry)')
>>> def nonoptimized():
        pattern.match("Hello\sCountry")

>>> def callonethousandtimes():
        for _ in range(1000):
            nonoptimized()

>>> test(callonethousandtimes)
The function callonethousandtimes lasted: 0.000645

>>> pattern = re.compile(r'/Hello\s(World|Continent|Country)')
>>> def optimized():
        pattern.match("Hello\sCountry")

>>> def callonethousandtimes():
        for _ in range(1000):
            optimized()

>>> test(callonethousandtimes)
The function callonethousandtimes lasted: 0.000543
>>>
```

Shortcut to alternation

Ordering in alternation is relevant, each of the different options present in the alternation will be checked one by one, from left to right. This can be used in favor of performance.

If we place the more likely options at the beginning of the alternation, more checks will mark the alternation as matched sooner.

For instance, we know that the more common colors of cars are white and black. If we are writing a regular expression to accept some colors, we should put white and black first as those are more likely to appear. We can frame the regex like this /(white|black|red|blue|green)/.

For the rest of the elements, if they have the very same odds of appearing, it could be favorable to put the shortest ones before the longer ones:

```
>>> pattern = re.compile(r'(white|black|red|blue|green)')
>>> def optimized():
        pattern.match("white")

>>> def callonethousandtimes():
        for _ in range(1000):
            optimized()

>>> test(callonethousandtimes)
The function callonethousandtimes lasted: 0.000667
>>>

>>> pattern = re.compile(r'(green|blue|red|black|white)')
>>> def nonoptimized():
        pattern.match("white")

>>> def callonethousandtimes():
        for _ in range(1000):
            nonoptimized()

>>> test(callonethousandtimes)
The function callonethousandtimes lasted: 0.000862
>>>
```

Use non-capturing groups when appropriate

Capturing groups will consume some time for each group defined in an expression. This time is not very important, but it is still relevant if we are executing a regular expression several times.

Sometimes, we use groups but we might not be interested in the result, for instance, when using alternation. If that is the case, we can save some execution time of the engine by marking that group as non-capturing, for example, `(?:person|company)`.

Be specific

When the patterns we define are very specific, the engine can help us perform quick integrity checks before the actual pattern matching is executed.

For instance, if we pass the expression `/\w{15}/` to the engine to match it against the text `hello`, the engine could decide to check whether the input string is actually at least 15 characters long instead of matching the expression.

Don't be greedy

We've studied about quantifiers in *Chapter 1, Introducing Regular Expressions*, and we learned the difference between greedy and reluctant quantifiers. We also found that the quantifiers are greedy by default.

What does this mean in terms of performance? It means that the engine will always try to catch as many characters as possible, and then reduce the scope step-by-step until the matching is done. This could potentially make the regular expression slow if the match is typically short. Keep in mind, however, that this is only applicable if the match is usually short.

Summary

In this final chapter, we have started learning the relevance of optimization and why we should avoid premature optimization by measuring. Then, we jumped into the topic of measuring by learning different mechanisms to measure the time of execution for our regular expressions. Later, we found out about the RegexBuddy tool that can help us to understand how the engine is doing its work and aiding us in pinpointing the performance problems.

Later on, we understood how to see the engine working behind the scenes. We learned some theory of the engine design and how it's easy to fall in a common pitfall—the catastrophic backtracking.

Finally, we reviewed different general recommendations to improve the performance of our regular expressions.

Index

Symbols

A

B

C

compilation flags

D

E

F

G

greedy behavior 19
groupdict([default]) operation 41
groupdict method 41
group([group1, ...]) operation 39, 40
Grouping
  about 53
  capturing 55
  operations 53
  parentheses () 53
groups([default]) operation 40, 41

L

literals 9-11
look ahead
  about 66-68
  negative look ahead 66
  positive look ahead 66
look ahead and substitutions 69-71
look around
  used, in groups 75
look behind
  about 71-74
  negative look behind 66, 74
  positive look behind 66

M

MatchObject
  about 39
  end([group]) operation 42
  expand(template) operation 42
  groupdict([default]) operation 41
  group([group1, ...]) operation 39, 40
  groups([default]) operation 40, 41
  span([group]) operation 42
  start([group]) operation 41, 42
match(string[, pos[, endpos]]) method 30, 31
maxsplit parameter 36
module operations
  escape() operation 43
  purge() operation 43

N

named groups 57, 58
negative look ahead 66-69
negative look behind 66, 74
non-BMP
  URL 50
non-capturing groups
  about 58, 59
  atomic groups 59
  using 88
Nondeterministic Finite Automata (NFA) 81
non-greedy behavior 20
normalize_orders function 37

O

overlapping groups 62, 63

P

parentheses () 53
positive look ahead 66
positive look behind 66
POSIX style support
  URL 7
pos parameter 32
possessive quantifier 20
predefined character classes 12-14
purge() operation 43
Python
  and other flavors, difference between 47
  regular expression, benchmarking with 78, 79
Python 3 49, 50
Python 3.3
  URL 50

Q

quantifiers 16-18

About Packt Publishing

Packt, pronounced 'packed', published its first book "*Mastering phpMyAdmin for Effective MySQL Management*" in April 2004 and subsequently continued to specialize in publishing highly focused books on specific technologies and solutions.

Our books and publications share the experiences of your fellow IT professionals in adapting and customizing today's systems, applications, and frameworks. Our solution based books give you the knowledge and power to customize the software and technologies you're using to get the job done. Packt books are more specific and less general than the IT books you have seen in the past. Our unique business model allows us to bring you more focused information, giving you more of what you need to know, and less of what you don't.

Packt is a modern, yet unique publishing company, which focuses on producing quality, cutting-edge books for communities of developers, administrators, and newbies alike. For more information, please visit our website: www.packtpub.com.

About Packt Open Source

In 2010, Packt launched two new brands, Packt Open Source and Packt Enterprise, in order to continue its focus on specialization. This book is part of the Packt Open Source brand, home to books published on software built around Open Source licences, and offering information to anybody from advanced developers to budding web designers. The Open Source brand also runs Packt's Open Source Royalty Scheme, by which Packt gives a royalty to each Open Source project about whose software a book is sold.

Writing for Packt

We welcome all inquiries from people who are interested in authoring. Book proposals should be sent to author@packtpub.com. If your book idea is still at an early stage and you would like to discuss it first before writing a formal book proposal, contact us; one of our commissioning editors will get in touch with you.

We're not just looking for published authors; if you have strong technical skills but no writing experience, our experienced editors can help you develop a writing career, or simply get some additional reward for your expertise.

PySide GUI Application Development

ISBN: 978-1-84969-959-4   Paperback: 140 pages

Develop more dynamic and robust GUI applications using an open source cross-platform UI framework

1. Designed for beginners to help them get started with GUI application development

2. Develop your own applications by creating customized widgets and dialogs

3. Written in a simple and elegant structure to help you easily understand how to program various GUI components

Python High Performance Programming

ISBN: 978-1-78328-845-8   Paperback: 108 pages

Boost the performance of your Python programs using advanced techniques

1. Identify the bottlenecks in your applications and solve them using the best profiling techniques

2. Write efficient numerical code in NumPy and Cython

3. Adapt your programs to run on multiple processors with parallel programming

Please check **www.PacktPub.com** for information on our titles

Learning Geospatial Analysis with Python

ISBN: 978-1-78328-113-8   Paperback: 364 pages

Master GIS and Remote Sensing analysis using Python with these easy to follow tutorials

1. Construct applications for GIS development by exploiting Python

2. Focuses on built-in Python modules and libraries compatible with the Python Packaging Index distribution system – no compiling of C libraries necessary

3. This is a practical, hands-on tutorial that teaches you all about Geospatial analysis in Python

Python Data Visualization Cookbook

ISBN: 978-1-78216-336-7   Paperback: 280 pages

Over 60 recipes that will enable you to learn how to create attractive visualizations using Python's most popular libraries

1. Learn how to set up an optimal Python environment for data visualization

2. Understand the topics such as importing data for visualization and formatting data for visualization

3. Understand the underlying data and how to use the right visualizations

Please check **www.PacktPub.com** for information on our titles

www.ingramcontent.com/pod-product-compliance
Lightning Source LLC
Chambersburg PA
CBHW082122070326
40690CB00049B/4178